Rushing to Sunset

Rushing to Sunset

HIKING IN THE HIMALAYAS (YOUNG) AND GRAND CANYON (OLD)

Judythe Pearson Patberg

Rushing to Sunset
Copyright © 2019 by Judythe Pearson Patberg.
All rights reserved.

To order copies of other works by the author - *We Just Shoveled Two Feet of Partly Cloudy, From Peace Corps with Love, A Winter Sabbatical, Tribute: Three Lives Remembered,* and *The Years Come and Go* - please contact: (Mostly) Minnesota Editions; 261 Stags Run; Harbor Springs, MI; 49740; Judythe.patberg@gmail.com

---

No part of this publication may be reproduced, stored in a retrieval system or transmitted in any way by any means, electronic, mechanical, photocopy, recording or otherwise without the prior permission of the author except as provided by USA copyright law.

The opinions expressed by the author are not necessarily those of URLink Print and Media.

1603 Capitol Ave., Suite 310 Cheyenne, Wyoming USA 82001
1-888-980-6523 | admin@urlinkpublishing.com

URLink Print and Media is committed to excellence in the publishing industry.

Book design copyright © 2019 by URLink Print and Media. All rights reserved.

Published in the United States of America

ISBN 978-1-64367-664-7 (Paperback)
ISBN 978-1-64367-665-4 (Digital)

01.08.19

Twenty years from now you will be more disappointed by the things you didn't do than the ones you did do. Sail away from the safe harbor. Catch the trade winds in your sails. Explore. Dream. Discover.

Mark Twain

Dedication

To all those, young and old, who crave adventure……. the kind of physical and mental challenge that inspires transformation and helps one to see the world a different way –

To my parents, who could never understand my wanderlust but gave me their blessing anyway–

To Bill, who is always there to support and advise –

To my sons and grandchildren, whom I want to reach the tops of many mountains, metaphysical or real –

Foreword

This is not a book to be read but rather experienced. Judy takes us down a path we will all eventually take, some earlier than others. Our finitude is brought into perspective by two of Judy's physical journeys……. years apart in time, but time only.

Most of our lives are spent, and I use that word purposely, doing things the world requires of us to survive. Yet, there are special times that, upon reflection, guide our lives and give meaning to our short time here. Judy's journeys are examples of those special times.

I have known Judy thirty years and am always amazed by how she casually brings up a past experience most would consider "something to lead with." Just this past year, when our families were together in Colorado, I referenced an avalanche that was on the news, and Judy said, "Oh, I've been in an avalanche before." After reading about the risks she undertook during the Himalayan trip, it is easy to understand how she can casually refer to an avalanche as a pesky intrusion upon her day.

While age does eventually take its toll on us, this book is a reminder that our state of mind and past experiences can help us through the difficult times and offset the ravages of time on body and mind. As the race to sunset continues, I'm not sure she realizes it, but Judy has already won.

The title for this book arose out of an experience last year when Judy explained to me the nature of the book she was writing. That day we decided to take a trip from Seattle to the San Juan Islands, and we wanted to arrive before sunset. The sun sets early in November on the San Juan Islands, and, as it turned out, we were late in leaving Seattle. We raced off the ferry, jumped into a rental car and sped across the curvy roads toward the western shore, and arrived just after the sun had set. Thus, the title for this book.

Steven Collier

Preface

This isn't a book about aging, but it could be. I am anxious about the aging thing. I'm not saying I don't want to get old (and older) because I want to live as long as possible and, since I can't live in a frozen state, I will continue to get older. My fear is feeling and acting old and – to a lesser extent – looking old.

I know people who think they're successful at "aging gracefully." Some are willing to give the credit to good genes which seem to slow down the aging process to the extent that the "you never change" exclamation is almost true. Others claim they manage the aging process by acknowledging the vicissitudes of aging and then choosing to focus on the benefits which, I admit, are impressive: the acquisition of wisdom, accumulation of life knowledge, attainment of long sought-after patience, celebration of freedom, and the appreciation of grace and joyfulness. They welcome a kind of quiet in their daily lives that they've never had. These graceful agers – in both camps– don't appear to need many different changes in scenery in order to be happy and content. They don't check their wrinkles or pay much attention to their aches and stiffness because these things are just a part of where they are and are not important in their lives.

While I embrace the philosophy of the second camp – and, to some extent, subscribe to it – I am not a graceful ager. It could be said that I actively defy the aging process by fighting against it, as much as possible. I check my face most mornings, and if my wrinkles are more obvious than usual, I slap cream into the crevasses in an attempt to fill them. If my legs groan or my hip hurts when I get out of bed, I try to fix the problem as quickly as possible by heading for the gym or going for a hard walk, forcing the pain to go away. Sometimes it takes a good mile before it gives up.

Does anyone else (over 65) panic when she's hit with the realization that time is not forever, that it's passing by so quickly she won't be able to do all of the things she still wants to do? I find myself reflecting on lost opportunities and a future that is no longer marked by infinite possibilities. I try to hold on to experiences so they can't turn into the past so quickly but, invariably, the cold, hard truth cannot be ignored: another year has passed, and I don't even know how to capture the sense of its passing. Birthdays don't work for me anymore. The sadness I feel is, at times, suffocating.

So, how is one supposed to age? Perhaps the best way is to do what many successful graceful agers are already doing: acknowledging the vicissitudes of old age while also affirming its benefits. But "acknowledging" and "affirming" are concepts that are too passive, too accepting, to be of any help to me.

Dylan Thomas's powerful poem keeps coming back to me, and I believe it encapsulates my spirit: "Do not go gentle into that good night; Old age should burn and rave at close of day; Rage, rage against the dying of the light."

Meanwhile, the aging thing moves ceaselessly, inexorably on………

This book is about two physical and mental challenges I undertook at different times in my life – one when I was young and the other when I was older but felt young. I was 26 when I trekked in the Himalayas for three weeks and 67 when I hiked from rim-to-rim-to-rim in Grand Canyon. In order to write about the Himalayan experience, I had to rely almost solely on the detailed journals I kept on my trek. Because the Grand Canyon experience is less than two years old, I could record the events almost as if they took place in the present. The Himalayan trek happened because I seized an opportunity to get off the beaten path, an opportunity that presented itself when I wasn't expecting anything. And Grand Canyon? I think I wanted to prove that my body could still work for me, that I wasn't too old for an adrenalin-driven adventure. I wanted another chance to face a challenge. Not surprisingly, I suppose, there are similarities in the adventures, probably more similarities than differences, despite the 41 years between occurrences. While the settings were different, the result was the same: I accomplished something that made me feel incredibly strong and good. I felt wonder and amazement at the ability of my body to endure magnificent challenges at both a young and an old age. Despite the hardships, I loved being able to climb out of my tent in the morning to greet another amazing day. For as many days as I have left on this earth, I want that kind of morning.

Maybe this book is about aging, after all……

Author's Note: Keeping journals of my adventures and experiences has always been a habit that I appreciate a great deal now, since my memory doesn't work as well as it did when I was younger. If it weren't for the journal that I kept of my Himalayan trek, I would never be able to tell the story, since the details left my memory retrieval system long ago. Because the Grand Canyon adventure happened fairly recently, the details are still quite fresh in my mind. However, I'm grateful for the journal that I kept during those six days because the entries helped fill in some gaps in my already fading memory.

I have intentionally altered the names and descriptions of my fellow travelers in both settings in the unlikely event they read this book and don't want my story to be theirs. What contributed to my sense of wonder and awe in the Himalayas and Grand Canyon may not be the same as that which contributed to theirs.

Judythe Pearson Patberg
October 10, 2015

Part One:

In the Shadow of Everest

Introduction

In an introduction to a book my mother and I co-edited, *We Just Shoveled Two Feet of Partly Cloudy,* Mom said that I grew up too fast. She said that, even as a young girl, I had a deep drive within me to accomplish a lot. I guess that must be true because, for as long as I can remember, I've wanted to "do things," and the things kept getting bigger and better. Lack of money was never a deterrent for traveling someplace I wanted to go….. neither was *naivete*. If there was any way to realize a dream, I would find it and then forge ahead with confidence.

There was a kind of restlessness about my traveling pursuits. I would no sooner end one adventure when I'd start planning my next. I must have felt the pressure, even at a young age, of living on borrowed time, so that I needed to experience as much of life as was feasible, given where I lived and the resources available to me.

I embarked on an adventure path that spanned ten years, from high school graduation to the end of my Peace Corps travels; took a thirty-year hiatus for raising a family and pursuing a career; and only resumed that path in the last five years. Even before

I entered high school, however, and during many of my boring classes while still in school, daydreaming about a time when I could begin to see the world became an all-consuming passion. I worked hard on creating a list of places I wanted to go and things I wanted to do before I settled down. I worked on that list until I was satisfied with my masterpiece. That list stayed with me – physically, in my purse or housed in a drawer–until I was well into my career, at which point I was able to check off all of the items except for one (work as an airline stewardess).

So, it should come as a surprise to no one that I agreed to accompany a medical student on a difficult trek to the Mt. Everest Base Camp with no training or hiking experience. I had terminated my Peace Corps experience in the Philippines and was taking the long way home to Minnesota. At the time of the invitation I was in Kathmandu, having left Thailand at the insistence of the Thai police who threatened to arrest me for visa expiration if I didn't leave the country. While the Peace Corps was on my master list of things I wanted to accomplish before I settled down, hiking in the Himalayas was a spontaneous decision.

But here I was, and that's where this story begins.

*We shall not cease from exploration, and the end
of all exploring will be to arrive at where we
started and know the place for the first time.*
                                                T.S. Eliot

For the five weeks after having left the Peace Corps and Manila, I almost went broke saving money in Hong Kong, witnessed destruction caused by the Vietnam War in Saigon, fell in love with a Peace Corps Volunteer in Thailand, and boarded a plane for Nepal when my Thai visa expired. My intention was to stay in the tiny, curiously remote – and almost unknown – country of Nepal just long enough to apply for another visa to Thailand, so I could re-join Bill. However, I was immediately fascinated by Kathmandu. The labyrinth of narrow, dusty, crooked streets teeming with old cars, cows, fruit sellers, bicycles, and people clothed from head to foot, along with sights, sounds and smells totally outside of my realm of experience, captured my imagination and made me want to learn about this country. For two days I wandered the maze of backstreets and smelled the sweet incense wafting out of stores and tallish brick houses with old dark carved wooden window frames and doors.

Now it was the end of May. On my third day in Kathmandu I found a friend. Ray was a Johns Hopkins medical student studying the needs of the Sherpas along the Tibetan border. He enthusiastically described his plans for a 30-day trek to Mt. Everest's base camp and invited me to go along. I questioned his timing because June is not the ideal month for long, difficult treks into the remotest areas of Nepal. The monsoons were about to descend any day, bringing with them the most despised of all hikers' enemies: leeches. Ray assured me that he had made adequate provisions for monsoon season and repeated his invitation. Common sense told me not to accept his offer – I was in no way prepared for the rigors of backpacking in the mountains – but my lust for adventure and new challenges won out. Besides, who wouldn't be thrilled with the prospect of walking in some of the footsteps of Edmund Hillary and Tenzing Norgay during their 1953 Mount Everest summit. So there I was – chaotically making the basic preparations for a brand new experience: trekking in the wild, remote Himalayan Mountains. Destination: Mt. Everest Base Camp.

On May 28th, Ray told me he wanted to leave Kathmandu on June 1st, so I had three days to get ready. He gave me his list, and I bought seconds of all the food he had already packed and some additional medical supplies. After hassling with immigration officials for a visa extension and a trekking permit, I traded my luggage for a well-worn rucksack and then set off to buy some much-needed socks. Dan and Roger, two Peace Corps Volunteers from India I had met at Aunt Jane's restaurant, warned me that this may turn out to be my most difficult task, and they accompanied me on my quest. It turns out they were right. After two hours of unsuccessful shopping, Roger stopped a man on the street and asked him, in Nepali, where we could buy socks. The guy waved his hands and said, "Oh, everywhere" in the kind of voice that reflected his exasperation at the ignorance of foreigners. An hour and several shops later, we evidently hadn't hit upon "everywhere" because I still had no socks. We were five minutes away from admitting defeat when I spotted the socks I wanted….. on the feet of a stranger walking by. We made eye contact, and he must have noticed my forlorn expression because he asked me if he could help. I asked him if he would mind telling us where he had purchased his socks and he said, "New York. Why do you ask?" I quickly described my plight and, before I could finish, he proceeded to take off his socks and hand them to me! I hadn't yet recovered enough to thank him when he waved me on and told me to have a good trip. The next day I saw Bob again, and he joined our little group.

My last point of business for the day was to change some money. I had only to think this when a Nepalese approached me and hissed, "Change your money – good rate." I hissed back, "Okay," and he took my hand and surreptitiously led me through a tiny door, up two flights of treacherous stairs and into a dimly lit room where the dealer hurriedly sealed the transaction (13.50 Nepalese rupees to a $1.00 traveler's check; today, one dollar equals 97 NPR) and sent me on my way. It was only when he opened the door for me and I got a better look at him that I realized he was the sneaky little bandit who made me pay 30 rupees and my suitcase for a dirty, smelly rucksack which he knew I desperately needed!

After changing our money, all of us rented bikes for a trip to Bodnath, the home of an impressive stupa and marvelous curio shops with all kinds of interesting treasures. Great experience and a lot of fun!

We spent the next couple of days exploring Kathmandu which has been called a beauty spot of the world. What I've seen so far doesn't match my schema for beauty, but the city is utterly fascinating. There are no driving rules! Green light means full speed ahead; yellow light, full speed ahead; and red light, full speed ahead and honk. The roads are narrow with no lines – drivers and pedestrians go wherever they want, and dare, to go. I feel as if I'm putting my life in danger every time I venture out into the streets. Busses, bicycles, cows, dogs, food carts, rickshaws, sewage trucks and trash – it's a crushing mess! The smog never disperses, and it's hard to breathe through the grit.

The city is crowded with beggars who should not be given anything (we were told) because giving demoralizes more than it helps. Besides, in many instances (we were told), racketeers have organized the beggars and skim off a large part of the take. And, of course, if you give to one, ten more appear, expecting a handout. Anyway, one six-year-old boy followed us for about ten minutes, and when we had distanced ourselves from the crowd, I slipped him a rupee (13 cents) which is five times as much as he expected. The grin on his face and the light in his eyes made it one of the best rupees I had spent so far. Okay, so the kid was demoralized!

Two men witnessed the handout and must have determined that we were easy marks for the hashish market. They took us to the "Dreamland Hashish Shop" which had no doors or windows so selling was literally wide open. One stoned fellow sat in the dusty entrance intoning, "Buy hashish. Change dollars." I could hear Dylan grinding out "It Ain't Me Babe" from the second floor of the shop.

The hashish shop looked the same as all of the tea and cigarette shops. We sat on stools alongside a friendly salesman who showed us a bar of stuff about the size of a paperback book. It looked like pressed ashes. He placed the hash on a balancing scale which registered one kilo and said he was willing to sell it for $80. One of the other Westerners in the shop smelled it, granulated a bit of it in his fingers and declared it a good buy. "It'll bring $1,000 in the States wholesale and ten times that much on the street. You should buy it," he said. I asked the salesman about the problem of bringing it back through customs and he said, "For you it would be no problem." I asked him why he emphasized the "you" and he said, "Because you people are doing the checking." I then asked him how long one kilo would last a person who had just an ordinary habit. He said he did not like the word "habit" because it suggested something sinister which it was not and when "squares" (like us) finally realized that there was nothing wrong with smoking hash (it's legal in Nepal) they would eliminate stupid laws against it, and people would be able to use it without having to pay such outrageous prices. He then answered my question that an "average" user would get two years' usage from one kilo of "good stuff."

As Dan, Roger and I were leaving the shop, stinging a little from being called square, the shopkeeper made one last attempt to sell us something. This time the merchandise was a piece of cake which had been seasoned with hash. There were about a dozen pieces being kept fresh under a glass dome. The Westerner said that if I ate it I would not remember buying it and within an hour, I would be enjoying beautiful thoughts. The frightening thing about the whole scenario is how easy it would be to get started on the stuff. Circumstances can make it seem so innocuous. Maybe I am square, but I know that a hallucinogenic experience is not what I need right now, so I'll be happy with occasional pot. Even that is off limits now......I'll need my senses and reactions to be clear and sharp over the next thirty days.

(I later learned that this scene took place on a street called Freak Street which was re-named in the 70s and dedicated to people who were part of a sub-culture that existed at the time......flower power, long hair, drugs, and Tibetan books.)

On our last afternoon in Kathmandu, Ray and I rented bikes again, this time for a trip to the Swayambhunath Temple (with a gleaming, white stupa) where a celebration of Buddha's birthday was in full swing. Legend has it that the Temple of Swayambu was created when Buddha, who traveled all around Nepal, turned over his rice bowl and died. One can't imagine the beauty – in song, dance, temples, ancient works of art, the sharp aromatic incense burning along with hundreds of candles, and people in worshipful concentration! The monks served us jasmine tea and Tibetan pastry in the temple. The deep-voiced chants, broken at moments by the tolling of a gong, put me in a hypnotic trance….. reality felt far away.

Tonight we'll have a last supper at Aunt Jane's. I'm going trekking tomorrow!

June 1, 1972

The story behind the famous Aunt Jane's American restaurant located on Freak Street in Kathmandu is about Jane Martin, the wife of a Peace Corps Director who had disappeared and rumored to have been murdered. She opened the restaurant in the late 1960s, offering hearty, home-cooked western meals that satisfied the cravings for North American food of Peace Corps Volunteers working in Nepal and those passing through. Everyone loved the sloppy joes (minced buffalo on an open hamburger bun) and chocolate cake with peanut ice cream.

After gorging myself on two sloppy joes, chocolate cake and a *lassi* (yogurt-based drink flavored with spices) with Ray, Dan, Bob and Roger, I went back to my 6x6 rat-infested room to wash my hair and body, using cold water in a sink. Ray came over for the fifth – and final – check of all the items on his list. I was already feeling nervous about the days ahead, and Ray's anxiety only made me feel worse. Would the monsoons hold off so the leeches stayed in their habitat? Do I have the right clothes for both tropical sun and sub-zero temperatures? Will Ray and I get along? (**Note:** It never occurred to me to question whether I possessed enough strength and stamina to get me through or whether I could actually do this with no training.) I wish Bill were here to talk me out of going, but he probably wouldn't do that even if he were here.

At this moment, I'm drinking boiled water from my canteen at the Koshi Hotel in the dusty village of Barabise, 14 kilometers from the Tibetan border and near the Bhote Koshi River. The sacred cows are helping themselves to vegetables in the bazaar. Of course, no one attempts to curtail the cows' activities, and they contentedly chew their tasty cuds. We left Kathmandu by bus early this morning, but not before I talked with some people from Los Angeles who were staying at the Yak and Yeti Hotel and were planning on going to Bangkok in a couple of days. I quickly wrote a postcard to Bill and asked them to mail it when they arrived in Thailand. Just writing to him squelched some last minute fears that overtook me an hour before our departure.

Our adventure began inauspiciously. After we boarded the bus in Kathmandu, Ray remembered some items he had left at Shrestha Lodge and had to leave the bus in order to retrieve them. I had no choice but to remain on the departing bus because all of our gear had been strapped to the roof. I survived a six-hour harrowing, heart-stopping bus ride that wound along steep mountain roads overlooking deep river canyons with rice fields. The driver, who couldn't have been more than 14 years old, actually turned around and was trying to talk to me as he crossed a narrow suspension bridge, hanging precariously above a deep gorge!

It took several minutes for me to calm my ragged nerves, but I regained my composure and smiled at our two porters, who looked a bit stricken themselves, probably more because of my white face and knuckles than the ride itself. Bucky and his brother can't speak English so, essentially, I am all alone, an oddity in this chokingly dusty village of strangely dressed people. I counted 16 earrings fastened to the ears of the woman closest to me. Her son, around three years old, is obviously suffering from malnutrition as evidenced by his little bloated stomach, dull brownish dry hair, and expressionless eyes. Ray said the air is saturated with tuberculosis, hepatitis, and malaria. The people are sick and make no attempt to refrain from coughing, spitting, and blowing their noses with their hands.

Nepal is a small, land-locked country, situated between Tibet (a region in China) to its north and India to its east, west, and south. There is a congenial blending of Hindus and Buddhists, along with other religions. Religious sects are not allowed to proselytize in Nepal, and the Nepalese are not permitted to change their present religion under threat of imprisonment. (**Note:** Nepal has been a secular state since 2007: Wikipedia) This is also the land of the Abominable Snowman, whose footprints continue to intrigue the world, and Shangri-la, which is nestled somewhere in the valleys of the Himalayas, at least so they say.

It is eight o'clock now and Ray just arrived. We ate a common meal of rice with *dahl* (a soup of lentils and vegetables), *chipatis* (a flat bread), and *chang* (a popular barley beer among the Tibetans and Nepalese). It was all delicious! After eating, we brushed our teeth, washed a layer of dirt off our faces on the street, and retired to our hotel room, which was a hay loft on top of the general store and restaurant.

June 2

We left Barabise at 6:30 this morning. Ray said that we conquered a grand total of five miles, but I think he must be a liar. Blisters on my feet, aching shoulders, and hunger pains constantly worked to remind me that an ascending mountain mile is much longer than an ordinary one.

The scenery helped to assuage my aching body. We passed through a series of narrow river valleys flanked by semi-tropical rice paddies rising thousands of feet above the river bed, hamlets surrounded by banana trees, and terraced hillsides. Rivers churned their way furiously through the narrow valleys. Enveloping all of this in their majestic vastness were the Himalayas – layers and layers of protective mountains. I was in a constant state of awe.

All day long, as we steadily ascended the rocky slopes, we met Nepalese singing their way down the trail. Their strong, clear voices produced music that wasn't especially melodious or harmonious. Rather, it seemed to tell little stories of joy, contentment, and heart-warming sadness. I was very happy to be in the audience.

Ray is a plodder and I'm a sprinter which makes us a little incompatible. I get so far ahead and then wait for him to catch up, slowly and methodically, never varying his pace. Bucky, our wiry little guide, and his brother, together weighing less than 200 pounds, are each bearing 65-pound burdens as if they were carrying straw. Ray is shouldering 40 pounds and my rucksack weighs a little less. Iodine tablets are a godsend for us because they allow us to drink all kinds of questionable water with a variety of unidentifiable floating objects. Our water consumption today averaged eight quarts apiece! Rest stops were short, frequent, and scenic. Our only food all day consisted of cookies and candies which we munched continually. Tonight, however, we feasted on noodles with dried mushrooms and canned shrimp.

Satisfaction and contentment are my lot as I watch while Ray washes dishes in a stream (we take turns). This is an enchanting land of mountain peaks that reach as high as the highest thunderheads and make me feel very small. I didn't know that such unspoiled – and overwhelmingly beautiful – country existed.

The day is dying slowly, and I'm sitting outside our tent, attuned to the sights and sounds around me. Far below, on the terraced mountainside, a farmer is still plowing by hand his little field which is one step of the terrace. A short distance away, the clang of cow bells can be faintly heard as a shepherd leisurely ends his day. I think he's having some difficulty persuading the sheep to stay separated from the cows. And he's singing, of course, in the clear, lilting voice which I've labeled the "voice of the mountains." I can only dimly see the two women carrying their baskets of wood as they slowly and firmly make their way to the little village above them. There are no stars tonight, so that means the flickering lights of the mountainside provide the only source of light. Soon the entire mountainside will be transformed into a small city with thousands of dancing fireflies – Nepal's rendition of "The Dance of the Fireflies."

A little girl has paused beside me, and she shifts the heavy load of wood on her back. She wants to talk but all I can do is smile. What a magical night!

But it's going to rain. I fear the monsoons are about to begin – and the grotesque leeches will attack.

June 3

How am I ever going to describe the events of last night! The rains began at 11 p.m. when all of us were asleep. Around midnight, I awoke to the sounds of hundreds of hands mercilessly battering the sides of the tent – wind and rain working simultaneously to unleash the full fury of Mother Nature. Before I had time to process that discovery, another one revealed itself in the form of three inches of water underneath our tent floor. The stakes were groaning in their effort to keep us grounded, and soon one was ripped from the saturated ground; then another succumbed to the raging wind. By this time, Ray had assessed the perilous situation and was frantically stuffing our sleeping bags, food, and other belongings into huge plastic sacks. The difficulty of the task was compounded by one whole side of the tent flapping wildly. The whole mountainside was illuminated by lightning, and thunder reverberated throughout the rocks and ridges. As far-fetched as it may seem, being blown off the mountain ourselves was a definite possibility. We grabbed what was left and then watched in disbelief as the last two stakes yielded to the irate elements. The tent sprouted wings and, like a giant parachute, sped downhill in the black night. The rain was plastering us from all directions – up, down and sideways. I was afraid to breathe for fear of drowning.

Ray and I blindly made our way to the overhanging rock where Bucky and his brother were struggling to keep our supplies dry. Our clothes bag had tumbled down the mountain, but we managed to hold on to our medical bag. For four hours we sat huddled together, not speaking the same thoughts all of us possessed: Was this a single storm or the first of a series for the next five months? If this marked the beginning of monsoon season, dare we go on? Could we return to Kathmandu if the rains persisted, or would we have to remain here? It was hard to imagine pursuing this adventure deprived of a tent and valuable supplies and, yet, I didn't want to admit defeat this early in the game. I thought, "God, this is also beautiful. A few hours ago, I was bathing in the glory of your handiwork, and now I'm trembling in the midst of your incomparable wrath. Awesome!"

At five o'clock, the rain had settled into a drizzle and the wind had abated. We stepped out of our shelter and, within seconds, our next hell began: The leeches descended *en masse*. They appeared to fly from the grass and bushes to viciously latch on to our bodies – every inch of our bodies. Without our iodine or salt handy, we were forced to pull them off, a process which left bleeding sores. I held it together until I covered my face with my hands and felt little leeches in my nose, ears, and even clinging to my eyelids. I began screaming and didn't stop until Bucky slapped me to end my hysteria. Then he calmly retrieved the salt from the jumbled contents of our medical bag and slowly applied it to the enemy, which extracted their final revenge by injecting an anti-coagulant before they released their hold, so that my blood wouldn't clot and I was left with a bleeding face.

At seven o'clock, the sun rose in the mountains, and this occurrence alone filled us with hope. Our clothes were drying, oatmeal was cooking, and we planned our day with no mention of returning to Kathmandu. I believe that we had experienced the worst, and this would prepare us for whatever lay ahead.

We didn't get started until 9:30 this morning because we had to search for our tent which we found, wet and torn, draped around a rock a little way down the mountain. It took a couple of hours to patch it and dry the sleeping bags and food.

For three and a half hours we scaled cliffs, rocks, and ledges. It was hard work with so little sleep, but our hardship was compensated for later when we entered a valley that proved to be a trekker's dream – hills and dales and Chinese-made trails (which means they're good!). Bucky instructed me, with expansive gestures, on the twists and turns of the trail and I set out by myself–free at last: three Thoreauvian hours of solitary communion with nature! Cuckoo birds and chattering brooks serenaded me all the way as I reveled in the beauty of the picturesque pastoral scenes.

Note: There are two routes to Everest Base Camp: through Khumbu Valley from the Nepalese side (southeast ridge) and through Rolwaling Valley from Tibet (north ridge). The southeast ridge was the route used by Edmund Hilary and Tensing Norgay in 1953 and is the technically easier and more frequently used route today because it's considered safer with better access to Mt. Everest. Climbers usually fly into Lukla from Kathmandu and pass through Namche Bazaar and Tengboche. They then hike to Base Camp in the Khumbu Glacier which takes six to eight days, allowing for proper acclimatization in order to prevent altitude sickness.

Trekkers who use the Khumbu route and other main trails to Everest Base Camp are able to trek in relative comfort with minimal preparation, equipment and support and the use of decent lodges along the way. No special permits are required. Even with the amenities, however, this route presents a physical and emotional challenge for trekkers.

The other route, through the Rolwaling Valley near the Tibetan border, begins with a bus ride from Kathmandu to Barabise and continues with trekking to Charikot, Simigaun, and Beding, ending in Na (less than two miles from the Tibetan border), the last Sherpa village of the Rolwaling Valley. From the

Rolwaling Valley, trekkers cross the Tesi Lapcha Pass and then descend to the Khumbu Valley.

The Rolwaling Valley is a wild, lonely, high valley called "the grave" by the indigenous Sherpas because it's buried down between steep ice giants. Groups of trekkers are not often seen, even in the peak trekking season. There are two factors which have helped to preserve this wild valley from the ravaging onslaught of tourists. First of all, it is relatively arduous to get there at all. Secondly, a special permit is required to be allowed into Rolwaling. Those who aren't scared away by those factors are richly rewarded with spectacular Himalayan mountain views and scenery that take one's breath away, not to mention mysterious stories of the notorious and celebrated Yeti who makes his home in the valley. (Information on the Rolwaling Valley was supplemented by Wikipedia.)

My trip was the remote Rolwaling Valley trek where the journey itself proved to be more memorable than my destination.

Ray is suffering from a malaria attack and I feel sorry for him. I think he's also depressed because he can't keep up with Bucky and me on the trail, and he's supposed to be a seasoned trekker. I try to slow down but I just can't accommodate his speed. Besides, I enjoy pushing my body to its limit. Ray's warning that I'll be paying a huge price for my fast pace later on does weigh on my mind, but it doesn't slow me down.

I'm glad we're taking the off-beaten, slightly-traveled trail to Base Camp: It's devoid of trekkers and signs of Western Civilization. But there's so much useless expenditure of energy in all of the up and down staircase climbing. Today we were, at one point, up 8,000 feet and now we're down to 6,000 feet again. The clouds are still above us, and the pine trees remain in the distance.

Since Ray was too ill to utilize his culinary talents or make it possible for me to put mine to use, Bucky cooked us a supper of rice and fried potatoes. He has a solicitous nature and tries hard to please. Both he and his brother are suffering from tuberculosis or bronchitis; they perpetuate a cycle of coughing and spitting. (The life expectancy here is 43.)

It's fascinating to watch Bucky eat with his fingers. He uses three fingers and the thumb of his right hand to mix and pick up the rice and potatoes which he brings to his mouth and flicks in with the back of his thumb.

Our sleeping quarters for the night happens to be another hayloft. I've been writing today's report, huddled in straw and mesmerized by the dance of a flickering candle. I wanted to sleep in our tent tonight, but Dave forecasts a downpour, so we opted for the "hotel."

June 4

We arrived at Charikot, our first major destination, at 11:00 a.m. after traversing and steadily climbing the final portion of a mountain. It was a decently challenging climb for any mountaineer. While munching on sardines and cheese, we caught a breathtaking view of the snow-capped Himalayas we were determined to conquer in the not-too-distant future. At one point, I commented on the clouds covering the tops of the mountains. Bucky used his limited English to correct me: the "clouds" were actually snow being blown off the top by 100-mile-per-hour winds. I shivered just thinking about the wind chill.

After celebrating our morning ascent, we embarked on our afternoon journey which took us down the other side of the mountain. And here we are–camped in a lovely valley beside a stream, smothered by pine trees and protected by the omnipotent mountain range. We're also at an all-time low altitude of 5,000 feet which means we've gained no altitude since we began this incredible adventure. I wonder when we are going to ascend to the great heights and stay there.

Any former ideas I entertained about the downhill being easier than the uphill have been crushed. It's extremely difficult and painful to descend at a reasonably slow rate; to do that requires practice on how to use one's legs and feet so they remain undamaged. Since no one told me how to do downhill hiking, I am now nursing blisters on the tops of both big toes, a gigantic one on my little toe, two on the upper part of my feet – and anticipating more to develop. I also have blisters on top of the blisters I suffered on my first day when we left

Barabise! My legs are in bad shape and, even though I'm on level ground now, I feel like I'm still going down. And I feel this way all because I descended too quickly with bad form……. Ray's dire warning has come home to roost!

This morning, while steadily climbing up our mountain, I left the group to enjoy a couple more hours of solitary communion with nature. The indolent butterflies and the cuckoos were once again my constant companions. I admired interesting rock formations and wild rhododendrons – even picked a cupful of wild strawberries which I ate hungrily. The land must be fertile because the fields were some of the healthiest I've ever seen. I stopped to "chat" awhile with a woman who was spinning yak wool. She milked a cow just so I could have a bowl of milk. We never exchanged a word during our encounter.

I love meeting people on the trail and offering the Nepali greeting, *Namasta*, said with both hands placed in a tent-like position in front of the face. Every so often I have the good fortune of hearing a *procenta* (singing group) in the distance. My heart soars as the group gets closer and their music becomes louder. They pass me by, and I listen until the last notes fade away. The effect is long-lasting and sweet.

The Nepalese are friendly, open, and proudly independent people. In the past, India has tried repeatedly to control Nepal and has failed because the people refuse to be lackeys – they will not tolerate condescension or bullying. One day I witnessed a scene in a Kathmandu bazaar where an Indian was ridiculing a Nepalese for his toke, which is the national hat. The Nepalese wasn't intimidated by the height and weight advantage of the Indian, and he fought fiercely until an onlooker – no, three people – pulled him away. The Indian retreated humbly.

By some wild reverse ecology, I ran into a little forest of Norway pines nestled on top of a small hill between two larger hills.

We dined tonight on a tasty dish consisting of fried potatoes, canned salmon, and lentils cooked on an open fire. A spoonful of jam sweetened things up a bit. Now it's time for a bath in the stream before darkness envelopes our lovely haven. I'm a little concerned about my blistered, aching feet – hope I can get them in shoes tomorrow.

June 5

I spent another morning in earthly paradise. As soon as we began today's journey, we found ourselves in a transition zone – emerging from the tropical rain forest into a land of pine trees and pungent air. Our most definable change was the snow-dressed peaks clearly visible in the distance.

The pine trees were like an oasis in the desert for a northern Minnesota girl. Reveling in their clean, majestic beauty and fresh smell while listening to the rushing waters of the river below provided all the happiness I wanted and needed. The trail was smooth and padded with soft pine needles, so I eagerly released my brutalized feet from the binding tennis shoes and slipped them into my sandals. They looked like war casualties with every toe wrapped in bandages and gauze plastered on the top. Ray had wanted me to buy some hiking shoes in Kathmandu but I didn't have enough money. Now I wish that I had sacrificed something else – perhaps the gifts I bought – for proper shoes because my feet hurt a lot.

As I sauntered along, intoxicated by the unspoiled beauty, I became acutely aware of the simple life these people lead and the absence of any significant concessions to modernism. Their way of life lends an atmosphere of agelessness to the whole surrounding. In that pine-clad river-fed valley high in the mountains, there is a harmonious blending of the ways of nature and those of man. The singing minstrels, the goat herders, the processions of heavily burdened people traveling from town to town to trade or sell their goods – all of these groups blend with the snow-clad peaks and snow-fed rivers to make the valleys of Nepal one of the most picturesque attractions on earth. As I follow the trail through forests and over rocks, uphill and down, nature exercises a wordless charm on my mind.

We rested beneath a huge pine tree beside a lazy brook and, while sharing my cookies with three stray goats, I reveled in my complete happiness, unaware of what lay ahead.

I have heard that one of the greatest challenges in trekking is that the trekker never knows where and over what kind of terrain the trail will take him next – unless he's made the trip before – so he can't be prepared for what lies ahead. That was the case for us. After our rest, the trail decided to test our skill and endurance. Huge sharp boulders and small slippery rocks along the river bed presented me with my first real hiking challenge. I was wearing sandals so I exchanged them for my tennis shoes, but I couldn't tie them because my feet were so swollen. After half an hour, the pain was so great that it made walking impossible and I had to put my sandals back on. At this point, I could only pray for help. Help came from Ray who picked me up when I fell, washed my cuts with cold water, and tried not to see my tears of frustration and helplessness. I'm sure he was tempted to say, "I told you so," but he never did. I was so grateful for his kindness and patience…….

I slipped, stumbled, and fell for three hours, despairing that I was doing irreparable damage to my feet. Just when exhaustion threatened my very survival, Bucky pointed to a swinging rope bridge that would carry us over the swirling, foaming water of the Tami Koshi River. Theoretically, it was supposed to get us across, but in my fragile emotional state I just knew that it would fail to do so. Bucky gestured for us to go. Ray was halfway across (I could see his whole body shaking) before I took my first step, then another. At first, the bridge swung silently and gently like a cradle. I closed my eyes and concentrated on placing one foot in front of the other; the platform which wrapped around my feet was no more than a foot wide. My confidence temporarily restored, I decided to meet the enemy in heroic fashion, so I opened my eyes and glanced at the erratic river, which was creating foam and froth several feet high while squeezing headlong through the narrow gorge. At the same time my eyes opened, the bridge started creaking and swaying faster. My sandals wanted to slip into the gaping holes where the platform had worn away; I gripped the rope on each side of me so tightly that my whole upper body burned. The thought that I would never see my family again crossed my mind, and it was horrifying. When my feet finally touched solid ground, I hugged both Ray and Bucky……. even Bucky's brother permitted a small hug. At that moment, I vowed that no swinging bridge would terrify me again.

As I sit here on a rock, a wee baby goat is licking my leg while its mother and numerous brothers and sisters hover nearby. Goats' eyes are interesting: white with horizontal black slits in the middle. The day is drawing to a close and preparations are being made for the night. Our campsite is once again a picturesque setting – green grass with grazing goats by an energetic river enclosed by three layers of mountains. A swinging rope bridge over the river (perfectly benign!), a farm house on the hillside, and a little shepherdess complete the picture.

Bucky is gathering wood for our campfire; Ray is setting up the tent; and I will soon be concocting a tasty dish of noodles, powdered eggs, and cheese that won't melt. We're at our all-time low altitude of 5,000 feet again. Bucky gestures that it's up, up, and up (moves his hands higher with each "up") all the way tomorrow so we should gain some altitude and, hopefully, stay there. The heavenly lights are being extinguished quickly, so I'd better get the cooking pot on the stove.

June 6

After waking up at 5:00 this morning, when the countryside was beginning to stir, I forced myself to eat Bucky's version of oatmeal (wretched, but it sticks to the stomach all day), which I washed down with an extra cup of our coveted coffee. I was mentally and physically prepared for the day which turned out to be both horrendous and satisfying. It was horrendous because we scaled a whole mountain, climbing straight up 2500 feet in five hours without food and water. It was satisfying because, for the first time, I felt close to our destination. Whenever I felt like I couldn't move another step, I'd glance up at the "Great Snowy One" which seemed to urge me on with a whisper: "Come on, you can do it. Look what's waiting for you, and I'm only one of many." Somehow I would summon my mind, heart, feet and legs, and together we'd surge forth. We had consumed our last liter of water about a quarter of the way up, thinking there would be springs along the way, There were none to be found, and by the time we reached the top, we couldn't speak for the thickness of our saliva. To have eaten without water would have been suicide so, at the end, we were a starving, dehydrated crew. I was fatigued to the point of feeling dead!

The trail was so vague that we lost it at one point and spent half an hour searching for a definition. We slipped and slid on a floor of dry pine needles, and twice I fell into a ravine. Both times, I picked myself up and examined my cuts and bruises nonchalantly……. this trauma was nothing compared to the swinging bridge.

The absence of people and human activity was very noticeable. I felt like we were trespassing on virgin land.

We met three Frenchmen with their porters and a Sherpa guide on the trail. One fellow had left his pack containing his passport, trekking permit, and camera on a rock. He had returned to retrieve it, only to find it was gone. I felt sorry for him. They had left Kathmandu a day before us; in fact, they had asked us what path to Base Camp we were taking so I wasn't surprised to see them.

Everyone hustled to set up camp before the lights went out. Our home for the night is a farmyard, and our hosts are the friendly chickens, cows, and goats. I'm watching with interest the scene that is unfolding. A wailing baby is encased in a box tied to a woman's back, and the mother is stoically beating the bottom with a stick, an action that only intensifies the little girl's crying. Another woman, kneeling on the ground is methodically grinding millet, and a third is washing a pot with mud and leaves. The children are staring with large round eyes, and the smallest one shivers. It is cold. The clouds are resting on the mountains which are visible in five layers. Looming over all of them is Gaurishankar, its snow-covered peaks sparkling in the last rays of sunlight. The sun is being filtered through the clouds, and its beams cast a heavenly glow on the mountainside. We're at an altitude of 7,500 feet and we're going to stay here. Tomorrow we should reach Simi, and then Beding which lies in the fantastic Rolwaling Valley.

Note: Gaurishankar is the second highest mountain in the Rolwaling range behind Melungste. The Tibetans and Nepalese believe the mountain is sacred. It has two summits; the southern summit is called Gauri and the northern summit Shankar. (Information from Wikipedia).

June 7

By now I should be describing a typical day in the life of a trekker, but it just doesn't exist. I remember talking about this with one of the Peace Corps volunteers I met in Kathmandu. He said that he had tried trekking in the Himalayas twice but didn't arrive at his destination either time. It was his dream, but the terrain was too difficult and unpredictable for him. I would add that trekking here is exasperating: One gains no perspective from looking at a map and distance is impossible to judge in terms of miles. Ray claims that the Himalayas offer the most difficult hiking in the world because it's all up and down staircase climbing whereas most mountain ranges have switchbacks.

This morning we explored an interesting piece of real estate, which took us into the remotest wilds of Nepal where there are no roads, electricity, plumbing, radio – the wheel hasn't even been invented in some areas! But its rugged virginity and infinite diversity presented a picture that was so beautiful it took my breath away.

For five hours we climbed up-down-level, up-down-level until we reached a cluster of about 100 homes terraced out of a cliff. This was the hamlet of Simiguan and, since it was noon, we decided to remain in Simi for the rest of the day so we would have a full day tomorrow to reach Beding, our next destination. Besides, we needed the rest. I washed my hair, soaked my feet, napped and read. Ray and I tried to engage Bucky and his brother in conversation. They spoke little, used gestures, and smiled a lot. Ray and I stayed up late, talking about our goals and ambitions. It was the first serious conversation we had since leaving Kathmandu. He is in his third year of medical school at Johns Hopkins and will use the data he's collecting on the medical needs of the Sherpas along the Tibetan border to fulfill a thesis requirement. He takes advantage of every opportunity to talk to Tibetan monks and people he meets along the way. Every night he records discoveries, ideas, and information in a journal. I can't figure out how he gathers his data, since he doesn't speak Nepali beyond a bare minimum. He even has trouble communicating with Bucky. I don't pry very much into his project and ask questions only when I'm invited to do so. He is very shy and very reserved. I appreciate him a great deal. He's given me this opportunity to experience something beyond my wildest dreams, and I trust him implicitly. I hope that we can remain friends after we part ways back in Kathmandu.

Once again, we've camped in the dirt yard of a farmhouse swarming with runny-nosed ragamuffins. Feeling their stares and listening to their giggles, I realize that I know almost nothing about the lives of these people – their troubles......the harshness, danger and suffering they face every day. Sickness and disease are bitter fixtures in their everyday lives. Everyone coughs and spits; even the children have already been inflicted with tuberculosis or bronchitis. I read that 50 percent of the people die before age five, with malnutrition and dysentery claiming a horrifying number of those lives every year. The primeval conditions under which they live blow my mind and make me want to cry.

June 8

We left Simiguan at 8 o'clock this morning, confident that we would arrive in Beding by nightfall. That prospect excited me to no end! Bucky assured us that this was a day's journey, so we pushed ourselves for a couple of hours and then relaxed a little – even stopped to pick a cup of luscious berries that carpeted the forest along our trail (Bucky didn't know what they were called but assured us that they weren't poisonous). Once again, I was impressed by the wild remoteness of this exotic country. I felt like I was one of the very fortunate few to ever set foot on its virgin soil!

During the early afternoon, we encountered and overcame a variety of obstacles, including every kind of man-made bridge imaginable. I met them all head-on, except for the rolling log version. Not even my conquest of our first swinging rope bridge – and all those that followed – could prepare me for the terror I felt while trying to cross the river on two rolling logs. I couldn't step quickly or precisely enough to keep the logs from turning so that I felt my feet slipping over the sides. At one point, I froze and refused to move. Bucky had to push me from behind. He kept talking to me and, even though I couldn't understand what he was saying, his calm, soothing voice propelled me forward until I stepped on firm ground. I think my body shook for a full ten minutes.

There was also the precipice we had to descend using a rope. That challenge appeared so soon after the rolling logs that I was still numb from fear, so I hardly knew what I was doing as I inched my way down the rope. Ray said that I performed in an almost robotic manner.

By four o'clock, Beding was nowhere to be seen, so we quickened our pace, stopping only when absolutely necessary. At six o'clock, Bucky was still maintaining that Beding was just around every bend and beyond every hill. We pushed forward and soon found ourselves in a thick, damp forest with darkness making the trail difficult to follow. Finally, we were forced to stop because our stomachs were aching and our energy was depleted. After shoveling noodles and tea, we donned our gear for the last lap of the journey, convinced that Beding just had to be very near. It wasn't, and our concern grew as the night descended upon us without any place to pitch our tent. At eight o'clock we lit some candles and silently began searching for dry ground. We didn't find any, so we pitched our tent in a murky bog while the biting cold wormed its way into our bones.

The next morning we awakened with sore muscles, congested lungs, and stomach cramps. With little conversation, we mechanically hit the trail again only to discover that Beding was, indeed, just over the hill! We had spent one of the most miserable nights of our lives a hundred yards from dry land.

June 9 and 10

My first discovery upon arrival in this long-awaited valley, which the rest of the world seems to have forgotten, was the presence of the lofty peaks, Gaurishankar and Melungtse, in full snowy dress. In the morning sunlight, they were fabulous! I saw "Buddha's Gaze" – the huge shrine painted with unblinking blue eyes rimmed in red that stare down at Beding.

The remote village of Beding is about two miles from the Tibetan border. At an elevation of a little over 12,000 feet, it is extremely cold. The scenery is spectacular and the atmosphere serene. The isolated village – mostly rock and ice – sits in rough, mountainous country, full of abrupt cliffs and pockets of rich pasture where cattle, yaks and goats graze. Houses are constructed of rocks, wood, mud and dung mortar. The air is filled with acrid smoke from fire pits, and the clouds are so close, you almost feel claustrophobic. Massive glaciated peaks surround the village, but Gaurishankar and Melungtse tower above all. During the day, these two peaks are shrouded in mist, and at night they appear cold and formidable. I enjoy them the most in the very early morning when they're arrayed in white shimmering coats – then they appear warm and beckoning.

Sherpas inhabit Beding and other villages of the Rolwaling Valley. They, like many Nepalese, are poor and appear sickly. The children look old with their wind-burned cheeks, weathered skin, runny noses, and tattered clothes. When I listened to them speak, I realized that they sounded very different from Bucky and his brother. Bucky explained that the language of Sherpas combines several dialects and is oral only. Sherpas are Buddhists and believe that the mountains are sacred. The Sherpas in Beding believe they are protected by a goddess who lives in Gaurishankar.

Note: Many people talk about Sherpas and porters as if they were the same people, but they are very different. Sherpas are a distinct ethnic group that migrated to the Everest region centuries ago and are well-adapted to high altitude. The porters come from the lower valleys and are just as susceptible to altitude sickness as are Western trekkers. Porters can be Sherpas living in the Everest region or Nepalese living elsewhere in the Himalayas. Bucky and his brother were Nepalese. We hired a Sherpa porter when we were at a high altitude and about to cross the glaciers. (Information on Sherpas and porters supplemented by Wikipedia)

As I sit outside our tent dressed in jeans, two shirts, a down jacket, wool socks and heavy shoes (which I purchased second hand a couple of days ago from a trekker who no longer needed them), I pity the little urchins crouched around our fire, barefoot and coughing. The penetrating cold is depressing, and I'm anxious to leave this place that Time has forgotten. One of the children offered me a potato, clutched in her little chapped hand. I accepted it and then gave her and all of the other children pieces of candy which brought smiles to their faces. I wish I could have given them all coats and shoes.

Last night a woman with pleading eyes and an infected knee came to us for the medical attention that every white person is expected to freely and competently administer. She took my hand and placed it on the throbbing wound. Ray and I accompanied her to her house which was a short distance up the mountain. The house was incredibly primitive – dirt floors, no furniture, and a cold hearth in the middle of one floor. Ray was able to make her understand that he needed water which she heated after struggling to build a fire. I washed her knee with salt and hot water and Ray bandaged it. We were about to leave when another woman appeared with a gash on her leg. Three hours and five patients later, we stumbled into our tent, weary and burdened with despair. It was easy for us to relieve the pain of an infected knee, but what do you do for a man who expects to be healed from the last stages of tuberculosis?

Ray, Bucky, Brother (he never told us his name, as far as I know), and I dined this evening on *sampa* and potatoes, the mainstay diet of the Sherpa people. Sampa is whole wheat mixed with water or tea and it's quite tasty. The only time Sherpas eat beef is when a cow or a yak "accidentally" falls off a cliff and poultry when someone else kills the chicken. It's hard to understand such unquestioning acceptance of deprivation when the effects of it are so visible, especially in the children who suffer from malnutrition. Sacred cows die of old age, whereas people die young.

I'm feeling sick and maudlin, and all of my thoughts – whether I write them down or keep them in my head – are depressing. The town monk paid us a visit earlier so we invited him to join us for a cup of tea. Ten minutes later, he returned, carrying a few potatoes which he shyly placed at Ray's feet. The scene was heart-wrenching, and I felt like crying.

My cold is worse, diarrhea rampant, and, all of a sudden, I'm very hungry. I could eat some leftover *sampa*, some powdered eggs, or pasty oatmeal but nothing appeals to me – only tea. Out of desperation, I mixed up some oatmeal cookies (guessed at the proportions) which we fried. They tasted like the dog biscuits I accidentally ate once, but they're filling so we packed them up to eat on the trail tomorrow.

One of the many lessons I've learned so far is that the necessities of life are really pretty basic. I don't mean to imply that we are engaged in a survival battle – *sampa*, noodles, tea, powdered eggs and pasty oatmeal are luxury items compared with the Sherpa diet – but there are times when I do feel that we are eking out our existence. I know that we are hoarding two chocolate bars, a can of crackers and peanut butter, and Nescafe for the time when we'll be battling the snow and ice – and Ray is guarding those creature comforts with his life! When I insist on breaking into the comfort pouch, he appeases me with a piece of hard candy.

It's so darn cold. I can't erase warm thoughts of home from my mind. Tomorrow we're bound for Na which is the last stop before the Teshi Lapcha Pass (18,700 feet). Ray dismissed Bucky's brother who returned to Kathmandu, and now he's looking for a Sherpa guide to take us over the pass, which is dangerous because of frequent icefalls and the movement of the glacier.

Suddenly, I'm able to interpret the strange feeling I possess about this place. It's as if I have been thrown into a Time Machine and spun back a thousand years. Nothing is familiar. Then there is the cold; it's unlike anything I've ever experienced (that's saying a lot coming from a northern Minnesota girl!). The whole country is a weird combination of the tropics and the arctic. The tropical sun burns my face and hands, and the arctic cold chills my bones until I can't stop shivering. Even though it's only 6:30 p.m., I'm going to crawl into my sleeping bag in a final attempt to feel warmth. I'll probably shiver all night.......

June 11

The journey from Beding to Na (14,000 feet) took us through three hours of wild, wild country with spectacular mountains swooping down on all sides into the glacial valley, which marks the end of civilization. It was light at 4:00 a.m., but it remained brutally cold until 8:00 when the sun finally began to emit some warmth.

At one point on the trail today, I felt something poking me in the legs as if it were urging me to move faster. Startled, I turned around, and an animal, the likes of which I've never seen, ambled past. It was black and white with long course hair and a broad horse-like tail that swung back and forth in the wind. This was my first up close encounter with the yak, the animal that is king of the Sherpa domestics because it can endure extreme cold. Yaks are aggressive and unpredictable. I remember talking about yaks with an older guy at Aunt Jane's in Kathmandu. He said that they always have the right of way on the trail, and trekkers should stand on the upper slope to let them pass or run the risk of being pushed over the edge. There's the story of two trekkers who stood on the lower slope of the trail to let a herd of yaks pass, and the yaks pushed them out of the way. Both trekkers fell over the edge and down the mountain. Since there was no medical help available, both died of their injuries. I also encountered a number of strange-looking animals roaming around on our trail that were half yaks and half cows (so I was told).

This is rock country and every man-made and natural object testifies to this fact. From our rock trail, I could see a number of potato rock gardens separated by rock fences. The houses are built by placing one layer of rock over the other and filling in the cracks and holes with cow dung. Even the roofs are made from slabs of stone plastered with sticks and dung. The only piece of furniture in the house we're staying at tonight is a rock structure in the middle of the room that's used for cooking. There is no chimney, so the smoke escapes from the holes in the roof edge. In one corner, a huge pile of dried cow dung is stacked to the ceiling. The people who live here are sitting on yak skins around the fire which is their only source of heat and light. I imagine they sleep on the floor wrapped in those skins.

Ray presented the woman of the house with a sewing needle, and she rewarded him with a broad smile. I watched while she separated the threads from a ball of raw yak wool, and now she is using that thread to sew a piece of cloth. She manipulated the needle in an easy and confident manner.

Immediately upon arrival at this humblest of homes, the children crowded around me as usual and commenced staring. Since I'm not feeling well in the first place, their heavy breathing, sniffing, coughing and staring unnerved me, so I brought out some brochures of Nepal I had placed in my pack as an afterthought before leaving Kathmandu. For one hour, these kids assimilated more knowledge of their country than they had ever been exposed to. They were fascinated by colorful pictures of Kathmandu and other areas of their beautiful country. I showed them their village on a small map, and they chatted excitedly among themselves. Although I couldn't understand them, I derived great joy from their new animation. The light in their eyes made them pretty for a while.

Tonight we dined on another Sherpa meal of boiled potatoes and yak milk with butter and tea. Our contribution to the meal was salt for the potatoes, which was very well-received. I can't for the life of me determine where all of us are going to sleep, but I hope I'm enlightened soon because I am numb with cold.

A misty cloak covers the valley and adds to its mystique. The high altitude is affecting me, making my feet heavy and my head light.

June 12

The mountains were fantastic this morning with the sunlight bouncing off their snowy sides, making the whole valley glow with the promise of a new day. I'm frightened, and for once in my life, I admit my fear. Ray and I discussed my state of health last night, and there's a strong possibility I'm experiencing symptoms of altitude sickness which are serious and, if ignored, can cause death. It's difficult to know which of my symptoms (coughing, nausea, headache, irritability, and light-headedness) should be attributed to my cold and which are a result of the high altitude. When I woke up this morning, Ray asked me if I wanted to return to Kathmandu, and I replied that I honestly didn't know. Now I'm faced with a decision, the most serious that I've ever encountered. I can appreciate how incredibly remote this area is – no medical facilities, radios, or help in any form if something should happen. If we had chosen the regular route to Base Camp, we would probably be near a hospital right now. As it is, we're at least five days away from anything that even resembles civilization – aiming for 19,000 feet of ice and snow. We're alone with God.

We left Na late this morning after discussing my condition. I decided to continue and, after our five-hour gradual ascent to almost 16,000 feet, I actually felt a little better. We are now a motley crew, having added a displaced Tibetan to our Nepalese-Sherpa-American group. I must admit that our new guy adds a distinctive flavor to our routine. A short while ago, he brewed each of us a cup of Tibetan tea (with salt and rancid yak butter), and only my long-established cultural sensitivity could induce me to finish it. After the tea ceremony, he assumed a yoga position and commenced chanting his prayers which were transported to Buddha via aromatic wisps of incense. The chanting ceased only when his rumbling stomach (I thought I could hear it above his voice!) forced him to prepare an all-time favorite dish consisting of fried potatoes, chilies, and dried yak meat which tasted like beef jerky.

My slightly improved condition didn't last long. I now feel as if I'm suffering total shipwreck with my ability to write down the sounds, sights, and sensations of this place where we've stopped for the night. Oxygen depletion has turned my mind to mush. My symptoms have returned with a vengeance....... my head is pounding and breathing is difficult. I'm too cold and too tired to think.

I'm in a strange world – a black, white and gray world comprised of a murky glacial lake with a border of white, rocky sand dunes and a moving mist hiding the solid wall of mountains. Between the small summit where I am sitting and this still-life painting lies a bed of white rocks spattered with black ink. The scene before me is deep, mysterious, intense and somehow, unreal – like a moon painting. That's it – I feel as if I'm on the moon!

Added to this moon effect is the unnatural but necessary slowness with which I have to move, lest I find myself short of breath after having taken a few steps. And it's so cold. Every few minutes, small avalanches of white rocks tumble into the lake. Permeating the damp cold air is the pungent smell of sage, the only part of this setting that warms my soul. Everything else dampens my spirits and makes me long for warm, midsummer skies. The mist lifted long enough to catch a glimpse of the glacier – very impressive in its cold countenance. Tomorrow I think we'll be trekking laterally along the left side of the glacier and probably camp tomorrow night on ice and snow before reaching Teshi Lapcha. Despite my worrisome physical condition, the glacier excites and motivates me to keep on……my destination is near.

June 13

We're in the process of moving out into the wild, white yonder, and many doubts assail me this morning. Because of freezing temperatures and difficulty breathing, I didn't get much sleep and feel pretty weak. Breathing difficulty, even while resting, is one of the more serious symptoms of altitude sickness. I'm cognizant of all the problems facing me, and my head tells me I should turn back. But my heart urges me to go on because the end is so near.

The glacier is dazzling this morning. It beckons me.

My microscopic experience in the ethereal Himalayas is rapidly drawing to a close. I did set out this morning, buoyed by the omnipresence of the dazzling glacier, presenting the final hurdle to my destination: Everest Base Camp, Everest Base Camp, Everest Base Camp……the words pounded my head and propelled me forward.

We walked for three hours in loose glacier rock surrounded by landslides. At 17,000 feet, my hands and feet began to swell. I could hardly breathe and felt waves of nausea come over me. I knew I was in serious trouble. My body wasn't right. Ray took my heart rate and said it was 200. It was when I became disoriented that Ray panicked. He put a paper bag over my head and got me down 1,000 feet or so, until I could breathe better. At that altitude, he handed me a sleeping bag, down jacket, a few provisions, and instructions to keep going and be careful……. "take everything slowly." I don't remember saying goodbye and thanks. According to our agreement forged in Kathmandu, in the event that I couldn't complete the journey, I would have Bucky's services and company until Beding; from there, I would be on my own. I remember wondering if I had enough money to hire a Sherpa in Beding. I allowed myself one last look at the glacier whose glorious heights I would never ascend and pass over. Bucky and I then turned our backs on progress.

Note: Breathing into a paper bag to inhale valuable $CO2$ stopped my hyperventilating, and most likely meant the difference between getting me to a safe level and dying. Ray, being a medical student, knew this. I had never been this high on a mountain before and didn't know anything about altitude sickness which, I found out later, is a condition where the body doesn't receive enough oxygen. It can happen at any level above 8,000 feet and gets stronger the higher you go. I'm not sure if I suffered from the danger of having my lungs rupture (pulmonary edema) or my brain swell (cerebral edema). There's no way to predict who will or will not develop altitude sickness. Ray wasn't feeling well but his symptoms were not as serious as mine. I later learned from seasonal trekkers about the importance of acclimatization. We probably ascended 17,000 feet too fast, without giving our body time to acclimate to the high altitude. I don't blame Ray or anyone else for my ignorance.

And now, here we are in "Moonland" again and thankful to have arrived safely. The return trip was horrendous – the constant rumbling of rocks nearly drove me to hysteria. At one point, Bucky and I arrived ten minutes too late to be victims of a massive landslide. The discovery left me trembling for an hour, and Bucky was none too stable afterwards either. My hands are still swollen and my head is pounding, but breathing is easier and I'm no longer confused. It is freezing cold – tonight we'll be sleeping in a cave.

Depression threatens my mental state, but I'm trying to focus on what I've gained, not what I've lost. Even though I failed to achieve my goal, all that has been mine during the last two week still adds up to a lifetime experience. I'm bothered by a question that will never be answered though: Was my decision to return necessary? Was this a test of my body or of my mind? I will never know the answer. What I do know is that I'm quite sure I won't have an opportunity to trek to Everest Base Camp again. A small part of me, I think, was never sure that I could complete a trek to the Base Camp using the remote Tibetan trail, but I never let that thought linger long enough to dissuade me from trying. Surprisingly, I'm okay with my failure to have reached my destination. I love trekking in the Himalayas and am very happy to still be doing it.

Bucky and I decided to rest for the remainder of the day. I took advantage of the sun's fleeting presence by reading for a couple of hours. When the more powerful mist-cloud combination rolled in, Bucky entertained me with colorful Sherpa stories about the mysterious Yeti of the Himalayas. By concentrating on his lively gestures and minimal English vocabulary, I was able to lose myself in the fantasy until it was time to roll out the sleeping bag. I remember reading about the Edmund Hilary expedition in 1961, the purpose of which was to find the elusive and fearsome Yeti, better known as the Abominable Snowman. The investigation negated the existence of any such human-animal, but the report didn't damper the enthusiasm of the Sherpas who love to tell gruesome blood-curdling stories of man-eating Yetis. Bucky swears that the Yeti comes down into one of the villages once a year and absconds with a fair maiden who is never seen again.

Just as we were about to crawl into the cave, we heard shouts in the distance. I yelled back, and in a few minutes three men emerged from the darkness. I was overjoyed to recognize Ed, a guy I had met in Kathmandu before we left. He and his two Sherpa porters had crossed the Teshi Lapcha Pass from Kunde on the other side and were on their way back to Kathmandu. They invited Bucky and me to join them, an invitation which we readily accepted.

June 14

Not only did Ed invite us along but, because of the light loads his Sherpa porters were carrying, they insisted on lightening my rucksack. I gladly accepted the offer because my leg was killing me. It was my left leg, the one that I had wrecked during that hellish descent at Charikot ten days ago. The hot, searing pain persisted so we wrapped up my leg and, using an ice pick for a cane, I was able to hobble along at a rabbit pace. We ate at Na and arrived in Beding around 3:30 p.m.

Bucky had been a wonderful friend to me for two weeks, but it was time to let him return to Ray who was waiting for him. I felt sad when he hugged me and said goodbye. I watched him as he walked away and waved when he turned around.

We are now enjoying the warm hospitality of a monk here in Beding. Ed is working on a project sponsored by Harvard, microfilming Tibetan books in monasteries. He is fluent in Nepali and immediately elicited an invitation for us to visit the head lama of the monastery. The lama has agreed to accompany Ed to Na for a list of books in his monastery there. This will mean an extra day in Beding to relax, something I need to do because I'm still feeling tired, lethargic, and depressed. I can't get rid of the notion that I could have kept going……that my medical situation wasn't as dire as to necessitate turning back. I'm disappointed in myself.

The pouring rain leads me to believe the monsoon season has unofficially begun. I promised myself that I would use the extra day to mentally prepare myself for the dreaded leeches.

June 15

Last night I slept in a monk's abode. Ed left for Na at six o'clock this morning, and I was ousted out of bed ten minutes later by our host who requested that I leave his premises for less holier ground. He said he had a full day of meditation ahead of him and my presence would be a distraction. The incense he was already preparing was bringing back my headache, so I was happy to move my body and belongings to a room he had secured for me in a nearby house. I settled down to a day of reading, writing, and reflecting.

I discovered among Ed's books *The Way of Life* by Laotzu and read about a simple philosophy of life written more than thirty centuries ago but strangely relevant to today's world, especially the one I'm living in at this time. About formal education Laotzu said that "people would be a great deal happier if they were set free with only their instincts and conscience to guide them." Really? If that were true, the Nepalese should be the happiest people of earth. And maybe they are. There does seem to be a lot of contentment in the short lives of the people in this country.

I was delighted to learn how healthy I am for "a man who knows how little he knows is well." That's me! I've always been aware of – and frustrated by– my limited knowledge in most fields. The more I learn the more I realize I need to know…….. this realization continues to be the cause of my burning restlessness for new experiences and discoveries. If I ever acquire excellence in any field – preferably one that involves strong people relationships – I must be a "real person" which Laotzu says requires "humility, sincerity, and a genuine caring for people at all times." These seem to be pretty basic qualities but I still come up short.

Laotzu says the possessions of a simpleton are three: to care, to be fair, and to be humble. Now I know that I'm a healthy simpleton! He also affirms that the best way to use life is through being. I wonder….. is "being" the opposite of "doing?" Is a person either a be-er or a do-er? Should there be more Marys in this world and fewer Marthas? I like the philosophy but it's a little vague to hold any real meaning for me, except to conclude that I probably should do less work and engage in more people watching.

Ed returned around 1 p.m., happy in his success at having obtained the list of Tibetan books available at the Na Monastery. I wanted to talk and he listened….. it was nice. I feel restless and out of sorts. I wonder what I will do when I get back to Kathmandu. I wonder what I will do for the rest of my life.

We have a whole day's journey ahead of us tomorrow, so I need a good night's sleep to replenish my energy supply. I just realized that the Nazi swastika is a mirror image of the Buddhist symbol of peace.

June 16

We bade farewell to the Rolwaling Valley around 7:30 this morning after a grand tour of the *gumba*, or temple, graciously extended to us by the head lama of Beding. I was allowed to look at the Tibetan book (hardly a book in the standard sense) in which is recorded the sayings of Buddha. I listened to Ed as he translated some of the sayings and found them to be very beautiful.

My feelings about leaving this cold, isolated, beautifully primitive valley included both relief and regret. Regret was the stronger emotion as I stood still and said goodbye to Gaurishankar and Melungtse, those lofty snowy peaks which now symbolize the unconquerable for me. The splendor of this wild, remote part of the world still fascinates me, but it no long captivates. I'm already thinking of this trek through the Himalayas as something that's in the past, an experience which has given me a great deal and taught me a lot, but which cannot induce the desire for more (at least not now). I've fulfilled a need which (unknowingly) had been a part of my life for several years: a confrontation between myself and nature. I know now – with absolute certainty – that I would be able to survive under the barest conditions anywhere with challenging forces working against me. But....... aren't I getting ahead of myself? I have to get back to Kathmandu and who knows what the return trip will entail –more challenges, I suspect.

As it turned out, the tortuous descent to Simiguan was almost more than I could bear. My leg, which was just beginning to heal, was put through the mill again, and by the time we arrived at our destination around 7:30 p.m., I thought I would be crippled forever. I couldn't even hobble the last 100 feet, so Ed had to carry me. And here I was arrogant enough to think that my experience was over!

While writing this to the beam of a flashlight, we're gobbling down our nightly after-dinner snack of boiled potatoes dipped in salt and yak butter. Our conversation has turned to leeches which we fear will descend with a vengeance tomorrow.

June 17

I woke up this morning startled to find the right side of my shirt soaked in blood. I knew right away that a leech had attached itself to my breast and departed sometime during the night. They were back – those dreadful vermin that suck their fill and depart, but not before injecting an anti-coagulant that leaves the victim bleeding. As we trespassed in leech habitats all morning, I became apathetic about the whole distasteful scene. When the vermin latched on, I brushed them off with salt; however, I missed a few that managed to enjoy my blood until they filled up and left on their own.

Five grueling hours on the trail this morning….. I could have endured them more easily if it hadn't been for my uncooperative leg, which made me groan and grimace with every step I took. Ed's Sherpas had chosen a trail which was different from the one Ray and I used, one that tried us to the very end of our ability and endurance. At one point, our trail was intercepted by a huge rock that was divided in half by a ledge. A quick assessment of the situation led us to conclude that we wouldn't be able to get around it, so we would have to climb over. The first part was steep and slippery, but I got to the top, crawling on my hands and knees and grasping whatever little root could provide some hold. After a two-minute rest on the tiny ledge, I tackled the second part which faced us at a left angle and looked considerably steeper than the first. I managed to conquer a third of it……then my leg refused to bend. Horrified, I realized that I was at the mercy of forces way beyond my control. I lost my balance and fell. A little tree growing out of the rock broke my fall but I still landed pretty hard on the ledge. At first I felt broken, but then I realized that my ample rear end had cushioned my landing, and I was very much in one piece. After steadying my shaken nerves and body and tightening the homemade bandage on my knee, I tried again and made it to the top. I applied salt to send yet another leech to its death, and we were on our way.

The afternoon was no less fraught with danger than the morning. It was around five o'clock, when a pouring rain was contributing to the day's misery, that we encountered another massive slate of wet, slippery, slanted rock that intercepted our trail. Once again, there was no way to get around it; we had to cross over. The left side of the rock ended in the raging, frothing river below. Since there was nothing in the form of a tree root or chinks in the rock to support our feet or guide our hands, none of us – not even the Sherpas–could think of a way to survive "the passage of death" (their label). We finally agreed to try Ed's suggestion which was to lasso a tall fir tree on the other side of the rock and tie the end of the rope to a tree on our side. We would then sidestep across the rock to the other side. After several tries, the lasso was successful, and Ed made his way over, followed by one of the Sherpas. Then it was my turn. Ed pulled on the rope to restore its tautness and yelled at me to go. With my eyes closed, I inched my way across. Halfway across, I thought I heard the churning river below and panicked. My hands slipped off the rope and I felt myself plunging toward the river. I grabbed an overhanging tree branch at the last minute and clung to it until I realized that I could use the branch to get to the other side. I made it across. While waiting for the second Sherpa to join us, I whispered a prayer of thanks for God's mercy which had been given to me twice that day. All told we had been at this for a couple of hours.

Even though the rain continued, I enjoyed the last two hours of trekking through gentle hills, cornfields, and a friendly forest. We laughed at some monkeys chattering in the trees, trying to make serious work out of their playing and at the cuckoo who insisted on serenading us. My heart lightened measurably as the signs of domesticity and civilization grew in numbers and frequency. Although I'm irresistibly attracted to the mountains, I feel more at home in the hills where the environment is less hostile and condemning… at least that's the way I feel now.

As I sit on a mat sipping tea after surviving more danger in a day than I care to ever experience again, I feel a wild craving for the world I know well, for people I love, for unreflective life – assuming that such life still exists. I'm touched by a longing, a sense of emptiness which I can't identify or even describe. I wish I could call for a helicopter, which would land somewhere in this mountainous terrain, and whisk me to Kathmandu where a jet would be waiting to transplant me either to Thailand or Minnesota. Instead, we're at least five days from Kathmandu and we're walking.

Before I retire for the day, I'm going to bathe in a clear, clean, refreshing mountain pool.

June 18

The word for today is monsoon. After sharing my sleeping bag with a multitude of bedbugs last night, and being compensated for my hospitality with sleeplessness and itching, I greeted the new day with bleary eyes, red active welts all over my body and dismal anticipation of more rain based on the overcast sky and interplay of thunder and wind. And rain it did – all day long as we sauntered through terraced pastures, and then quickened our pace through dark, dank forests and slowed down again while picking our way carefully over the riverbed rocks which caused me so much grief several days ago when I was wearing sandals. I discarded my heavy shoes and jeans and donned comfortable tennis shoes and cut-offs. The coolness and cleansing power of the rain was welcomed – in no way did it dampen my solitary happiness. I sang to my heart's content, running the spectrum of subjects – love, life, sorrow, happiness, home and God. At times, I thought my soul would burst with joy.

We arrived at our resting place, drenched and chilled, so we immediately built a fire and changed our clothes. I discovered that blood was seeping through my tennis shoe, and that could mean only one thing: A leech had worked its way through my shoe string hole and, attaching itself between my toes, had feasted to its satisfaction and departed (where to, I can't figure out). Sneaky bastard! I hate it when they gorge themselves on my blood and leave without being discovered. The reason I can't feel them when they bite into my skin is because, not only do they inject an anti-coagulant which induces bleeding, but also a painkiller which numbs the area so I'm not aware of their presence. How could God create such a vile, despicable creature and provide it with an ingenious means of survival! I think I'd better wear my chunky shoes tomorrow.

Ed and I had a long discussion about God and religion last night. He's got the same hang-up most intellectuals possess……. can't believe in someone or something whose existence can't be proven.

June 19

We came to Charikot Hill, saw it, and conquered it in four hours! This record-breaking time was a result of determination and a reluctance to stop once we started for fear that we'd never get up again. Last night was horrendous! I could feel hundreds of bedbugs biting every inch of my body, and all I could do was count the hours until dawn when I would be able to survey the damage. I am now peppered with huge, red, itching welts that show no sign of disappearing. Two sleepless nights have taken their toll, and I'm very tired. Unfortunately, my right leg has also adopted "Sahib's Knee," so I have to use two homemade walking sticks now. Ed's physical condition is not much better than mine, but we both derive comfort from the fact that we're out of leech territory.

We dined on dried wheat soaked in black tea at a fly-infested house. The flies irritated my bedbug bites, and I found myself climbing the walls.

June 20

We pushed ourselves this morning, knowing we had handicaps to overcome. Mountain trekking is hard work when all external factors are on your side, but when you're handicapped, it's very tough. I had to revise my climbing technique to accommodate my battered legs. Instead of meeting the hill head on, sometimes on all fours, and scaling it mountain goat style, I accepted it as an enemy that would be with me for some time, and engaged in a slow, steady process of small, plodding steps. I set my pace and maintained a kind of rhythm……. methodical and even mechanical (reminiscent of the days when Ray would implore me to slow down, and I ignored his advice, suffering the consequences later).

This afternoon I enjoyed a wonderful sense of well-being. My legs felt a little better – they seemed to adjust to the fact that they no longer had to work so hard. Not having to concentrate on the trail allowed me to lose myself in another world – the world of home. My daydreams dwelt on the joy of meeting my family again – eating simple suppers together and sharing experiences with them. It's been over two years since I saw everyone on the farm, and I miss both the people and the place. I was so relaxed in my serene environment that I almost fell asleep while walking.

It's evening and I don't know quite where we are – somewhere between Charikot and Barabise. Our plan is to arrive in Barabise tomorrow night, stay the night, and reach Kathmandu by bus the next day. My state of existence right now is unimaginable – for some reason, my body has reacted violently to the excessive bedbug poison so now the bedbug bites are covered with a thick, bumpy rash which also itches. I feel like I'm on fire. To scratch would be suicidal, so I pace the ground and bite my lip. I'm so miserable……. and so homesick. (And I'm whining way too much!)

June 21

This morning I awakened feeling refreshed and raring to go. Ed gave me a Benadryl last night, hoping the antihistamine would calm the allergic rash and give me a few hours of much-needed sleep. I slept so soundly that Ed had a hard time rousing me when it was time to leave. The rash and the bites – the whole itching mess is still with me, but at least nothing was added last night.

I did not daydream on the trail this morning. It warranted close attention and an incredible amount of exertion. We plugged uphill most of the way – gradual incline with no steps or level spots. A bridge that was supposed to be there wasn't, and our Sherpa made it clear that the only way we could continue was to climb up a waterfall. I couldn't believe what

I was hearing! I had already met terror several times and now it was challenging me once more. My fears turned out to be largely unsubstantiated, however. Climbing up that waterfall wreaked further havoc on my already damaged legs, but it really wasn't very dangerous or terrifying.

We stopped to rest at a house just below the pass. As usual, the woman of the house gave Ed a song and dance about her ailments. He listened and, since he speaks fluent Nepali, was able to communicate with her. He presented her with an aspirin and instructions to take it with water before she went to bed. Talk about medicine quackery – we've dabbled in it since the beginning of this trip. Poor people……. I wish we could really help them.

All I could think of while resting was our plan: Walk through the pass, over the ridge, and downhill all the way to Barabise, our nightfall destination.

There was only one emotion I felt when we finally staggered into Barabise around 8 o'clock tonight – beating the thunderstorm by one full minute – and that was relief. I was so glad it was over. We completed a three-hour run down the mountain in one hour. My legs became mercifully numb as I ran with clenched fists and reserved stamina I didn't know I had. When I realized we wouldn't make Barabise by nightfall if I coddled my Sahib's Knees, I took a deep breath and asked God to get my legs down the mountain. He did. The Sherpas and Ed were convinced that I was possessed by the devil; the Sherpas muttered their mantras while Ed struggled to keep up.

Breathless and spent, the four of us stumbled into the hotel and Ed gasped, "Coca Cola!" As I drained the Coke bottle, I said to no one in particular, "Am I really glad to be back?" I'll answer this question tomorrow. Right now I'm going to enjoy some rice, *dahl baht* and boiled potatoes. Then I'll wash my diseased body and sleep for as many hours as I can. Tomorrow morning, we'll be bound for Kathmandu via bus or jeep.

June 22

What a strange feeling it was to ride the bus to Kathmandu this morning, after having not seen anything that resembled a vehicle for three weeks. We arrived at eleven o'clock, and my first order of business was a trip to the American Embassy where I found letters waiting for me, one from Mom and another from Bill. I was relieved to read that everyone was fine at home and they were waiting for me. Mom asked me if I had been in trouble a few days ago and if I was okay now. She said she spent a whole night praying for my safety. As far as I could tell, her prayer date matches the times I was facing rock encounters. I have never doubted the power of my mother's prayers, and I wasn't about to start doubting now.

Bill wants me to return to Thailand (joy!). After a hearty meal (cheeseburger, chocolate cake, and a *lassi*) at Aunt Jane's, I rushed to the Thai Embassy and applied for a thirty-day visa which will be granted tomorrow. I then proceeded to Thai International Airlines where I was told that a ticket to Bangkok would cost $132. Bad news, indeed, since my total worth amounted to less than $100. The ticket agent, noting my distress, asked me how old I was and when I told him, he suggested that 26 might not be too old to apply for a student discount and asked me to come back later. It felt good to have someone working for my cause.

My next stop was the Peace Corps Office where I cornered the doctor to see what he could do about my skin disease which was slowly driving me crazy. Alas, he confirmed my suspicions that nothing could be injected or taken orally to make the lumpy rash disappear. His only action was to prescribe an ample supply of Calamine lotion to alleviate the itching and Benadryl to promote some peaceful hours of sleep without scratching. "One comforting thought about skin irritations," he said, "is that they always go away in time."

A return trip to the airlines revealed two silver linings: a 50 percent chance of qualifying for a student discount, which would reduce the fare to $100 and a strong possibility of boarding a plane for Bangkok on June 26th, Bill's birthday. There was still the problem of not having enough money for my fare……$15 short. My excitement at the thought of seeing Bill again was overwhelming, so I impulsively told the ticket agent I would sell my rucksack to him for $15. A look of bemusement crossed his face, and he said,

"I don't think that would be a good idea. You'll need your pack to get your stuff home. Be here at 2:00 tomorrow. I'll have your ticket ready." I thanked him profusely and left with a song in my heart. I would be seeing Bill again, lumpy rashes and all!

I can't believe I'm listening to an old Supreme album at the Shrastha Lodge. Tomorrow I'll pay a visit to John and Peter. I hope they've finished my "Wheel of Life" on white satin. It should be beautiful.

June 23

Sleep evades me tonight – guess it's a combination of my itching skin condition, excitement at the thought of being with Bill again, and just plain restlessness over things past and yet to come. My mind dwells on the incredible adventure that just ended and the many things I learned about life, God, nature and myself. Even though I was aware all along how unique and incomparable my experience was, it may be the case that it will hold even more meaning for me in retrospect. Sometimes distance and time are the only way we can fully appreciate the importance, gravity and beauty of a traumatic experience. At various times during this day, I found myself disbelieving that these three weeks really happened – it still feels like a fairy tale. People here think that my adventure was a fantastic act of courage for a woman. The owner of Aunt Jane's said that, in his twenty years in Kathmandu, he had never heard of a woman undertaking the challenge of an off-beaten, remote trek to Everest Base Camp. I so wish I had made it!

Here's what I think. I think that my experience required the following: physical endurance, mental and emotional stamina, a craving for rugged adventure and unexplored boundaries, the ability to endure long periods of loneliness, the capacity for silence and solitary communion with nature, a love for exhilarating fulfillment at the end of each hard day, and a determination to survive under any conditions. I don't think that all of this adds up to unusual courage, but rather it equals an insatiable love for all kinds of experiences totaling the whole of life. I know I have that – always have.

A Peace Corps Volunteer asked me if my trekking experience taught me anything about myself that I hadn't known before. I found that question interesting. During the two years I lived in the Philippines as a PCV, I overcame some challenges that made me realize I possessed a kind of physical and mental toughness. I think that my Himalayan experience only provided further evidence that this is true. I also am convinced that I can survive – even thrive – with the very basic necessities of life. Give me some potatoes, wheat or rice lentils, and a cup of tea every day and my existence is guaranteed.

I fell in love with nature – its fantastic diversification and destructive powers. I'll never forget the solemn beauty of glorious mountain mornings, when I would rub the sleep from my eyes and study the scene before me. The glacial lake would be lying motionless, a murky gray. Further off would be the mountain, its sharp jagged snow-clad peak dazzling in the splinters of morning sunlight, which hadn't yet reached the valley below. In a few minutes the sun would appear over the crest and illuminate the valley and lake until the whole world became one of light, pregnant with the promise of a new day and holding mysteries yet to be unfolded by those who live it. And in the silent and cold grandeur of this daily occurrence, I would feel the formal dignity of the strange mountain world which, in its cruel remoteness, refuses to meet man halfway but invites him to be challenged in a place where he is a trespasser and only sometimes tolerated in this role. During this moment of each day, I would submit to the burning desire to pay homage to God who created the sun, those mountains, the lake, and the sky –life itself. I'll always remember walking through treeless wastelands of white, moving rocks and listening to the rumblings of avalanches all through the night. I'll never forget the mind-blowing magnificence of the glaciers – how beautiful, wild and unspoiled it all was. And I'll never forget the awesome promise that was born in every mountain morning.

I know this is going to sound melodramatic, but I'll say it anyway: I experienced what it's like to fear death. When I couldn't breathe and my heart felt as though it would leave my chest at an altitude of 17,000 feet, I was terrified. I remember thinking how powerless I was to alter the situation. I remember thinking that if I did require medical attention, there was no doctor or hospital nearby to administer it. I worried that I would die.

But even more strongly felt than the fear of dying was the determination to live so that I could experience more of this extraordinary world God created. I also felt a certain amount of resignation toward dying....... an acceptance of its inevitability. I remember thinking that if I had to die I hoped it would be possible for my family to know how much I loved them. I worried about how that message would get to them.

Deep down (very deep), I don't mind that I never reached my destination. For me, the journey was more important than the destination. It was each step along the way, the magnificent beauty, the lessons I learned – that's what I loved.

I'm pretty sure there will be more adventures in my life. They won't necessarily take place in the mountains, although I feel as if I want to give mountains another try. Mountains bring out the best and the worst in a person. They are unforgiving, intimidating, and impersonal. I liked to climb them because they forced me to push my limits and deal with risks. As far as risks go, however, I never really thought about them much.

Beautiful women from Barabise whom we greeted on the trail

One of our nicer hotels. I slept in the part on the left, which also housed the animals.

Yaks – those ornery, frightening bad smelling animals we encountered on the trail

Simiguan, the first Sherpa village in the Rolwaling region.

Buddha's Gaze, the huge shrine that stared down on us at Beding – very imposing.

Back to Bangkok and Home

I boarded a plane for Bangkok on June 26th, Bill's birthday, after having sent him a letter from the Kathmandu Peace Corps office. I was excited to see him but also felt a little apprehensive because I had no money to get me from Bangkok to Petchburi where he lived. Characteristically, I believed that things would work out…….. *bahala na* (a favorite Filipino phrase; it means "leave it to God").

It didn't take long to find a bus driver who consented to giving me a ride to Petchburi with the few *baht* I found in the pocket of a skirt. However, he changed his mind when his supervisor overheard our conversation and forbade him to allow me to ride with inadequate fare. I had no choice but to hitchhike.

I had walked about a quarter of a mile when a truck stopped and the driver motioned for me to get in. We had driven only a few miles when the man stopped at a road side motel and motioned for me to get out. When I refused, he produced a gun which made me think that I couldn't stay in the truck. My mind was racing as he babbled in Thai and I pleaded for my release in English. I could tell by his impatient demeanor that he was not going to let it happen. When he opened the door to the motel room, he motioned for me to take off my clothes. I pretended to begin the process and he, in turn, laid the gun on the dresser in order to disrobe. Without thinking of the consequences of a violent act, I grabbed the gun off the dresser, ran outside, and threw it as far from me as I could. I continued to run, buttoning my shirt with one arm and waving with the other. Perhaps Mom was praying for me again because, at that moment, a bus stopped on the road in front of me. My attacker, who had picked up the gun and was chasing me, immediately hid his weapon and walked back to the motel. I boarded the bus, offered the driver my insufficient funds which he accepted (probably on the basis of my appearance which was likely to generate pity), and found a seat amid the chickens, pigs and inquisitive people.

The bus stopped at the Petchburi market where I had met Bill a month ago. I got off after thanking the driver profusely for his generosity. I realized that I still had to get to the college where Bill taught and lived. My only hope lay in the rickshaw drivers who descended upon me *en masse*. When I successfully communicated – through gestures – that I had no money, most of them left. But one remained. I told him, as best I could, that I would write him an I.O.U if he would take me to the college. Not understanding, but perhaps intrigued (and, certainly, compassionate), he agreed to take me. I cannot begin to express my discomfort at having this little man peddle me all the way to the college. I must have outweighed him by fifty pounds! When we arrived (he was sweating), I actually produced an I.O.U that said I owed him a fare. Nodding and smiling, he accepted the piece of paper. I had him write down his name and left to find Bill's house. (I found the driver the next day and paid him.)

I found the house with a note attached to the door. Bill had gone to Bangkok for the week-end to celebrate his birthday! This was not written to me (obviously, he had not received my letter) but to anyone who would be interested in his availability. The door was locked. By this time, I was tired and more than a little crabby (the itching had started again….. probably from sweating), and definitely not really caring about propriety, so I broke a window which allowed me access to his house. I located a bed and immediately went to sleep.

And that's how Bill found me the next morning: sound asleep, covered with hives and rashes.

We enjoyed a couple of weeks in Petchburi and Bangkok, falling more in love each day we were together. As I remember it, Bill asked me to marry him at the top of the Arawana Hotel. (This was the same hotel where I had embarrassed him by asking the waiter to take my steak back and cook it more.)

Bill denies the marriage proposal; he remembers a different time and place. I guess the years have changed our memories; either that or we each choose to remember it the way we wanted it to go. Anyway, we had a great time. I watched Bill teach English to college students, and at night we rode his motorcycle around to various romantic destinations, one of which was the market where we satisfied an intense hunger for sticky rice stuffed in banana leaves.

Alas, I had to go home. Since I had no money, Bill used a portion of his Peace Corps allowance (the portion that was left after our heavy spending) to buy me a ticket on the black market that would get me as far as Rome. There, the plan was for me to meet a man who would give me the second half of my ticket to New York.

When I arrived in Rome, I got off the plane to find a swarthy little man hissing and motioning to me. "Looking for a ticket to New York?" When I told him that I was the person, he handed me the ticket and collected a fare which was considerably less than a commercially (and legally) purchased ticket.

I found my gate for the plane to New York and felt good about my life. The plan was for me to introduce myself to Bill's parents and, hopefully, spend a couple of days with them so they could get to know me a little. Bill had written a letter of introduction which I carried in my purse and was supposed to present to his parents when I arrived.

Well, I arrived at JFK without enough money to hire a taxi to take me to Cranford, New Jersey where Bill's parents lived. It was late at night, and I was tired so I locked my rucksack to a bench in the airport and fell asleep. I was awakened by a cab driver who asked me where I was going. When I told him my destination, he offered to take me since he was going in the same direction. I thanked him when he deposited me at 317 Willow Street in Cranford and offered to pay him for part of the fare. He declined and wished me luck. I watched him drive away, feeling alone and very nervous.

Mrs. Patberg answered the door and I presented her with the letter from her son. "This will explain my presence," I told her. She invited me in and I watched while she read the letter. Mr. Patberg had entered the room by this time, and she said, "Pat, this is Judy Pearson, a very special friend of Bill's. She's going to stay with us for a while." I felt welcomed……. and was able to breathe again.

I stayed with the Patbergs for a week, instead of the intended couple of days. They hosted a party in my honor so I met all of their friends. I bought a leopard skin hat at Saks Fifth Avenue and enjoyed walking around New York.

But I wasn't home yet. I called my parents and told them to expect me in a few days. A week later, I boarded a bus heading west with a ticket in hand that would take me to Grand Forks, North Dakota, the closest to home I could get with my money (if I had used what money I had to hire a taxi in New York, I wouldn't have made it that far). When I arrived in Grand Forks, I called my parents who picked me up at the bus station four hours later. Three hours of driving and I was home on the farm. I remember savoring the observation that nothing had changed on the farm in the two plus years I had been away.

Part Two

Rim-to-Rim-to-Rim

Introduction

Fast forward forty one years. Having raised three sons, written several books, and ended a 30-year career as a university professor, I desperately needed an adventure, a physical challenge. I wanted to see what my 67-year- old body could do. Always a walker, I stepped up my exercise routine to include intense cardio and strength training in preparation for an extreme adventure I hadn't yet identified. Thru-hiking the Appalachian Trail (hiking the entire trail in less than a year) was an idea that germinated in my fifties and grew with the devouring of books about people who have hiked it, or parts of it. What I gradually came to realize, however, was that I wouldn't be satisfied hiking just a portion of it; it had to be the whole thing – 2100 miles from Georgia to Maine, which would take at least five months. Since I didn't want to be away from my family that long, a thru- hike was out of the question, and so was the Appalachian Trail.

Still training for an as yet unidentified adventure, I conducted a serious internet search and found what I knew would be perfect: Grand Canyon! A company called "Just Roughin' It Adventure Company" popped up on my screen. I decided to hire one of its guides when I read the following: "Travel in Grand Canyon has inherent risks and unavoidable hazards..... If you have doubts as to your ability to hike safely in Grand Canyon, do not attempt to do so! Be prepared to acknowledge the risks and challenges of stepping below the rim in Grand Canyon. And remember, hiking in is optional; hiking out is mandatory."

I was ready for a second experience of my lifetime.

Your biggest challenge isn't someone else. It's the ache in your lungs and the burning in your legs, and the voice inside of you that yells, "CAN'T," but you don't listen. You just push harder. And you hear the voice whisper, "can." And you discover that the person you thought you were is no match for the one you really are.
Unknown

Grand Canyon: Background Information

I'm convinced that Grand Canyon is the most spectacular, unique natural wonder of the world. Its sheer size overwhelms my senses: 277 river miles long, 18 miles wide, and a mile deep. Then, there's the rugged landscape – featuring a desert deep in the canyon and a diverse forest of coniferous trees at its North Rim – and the stunning sequence of rock layers that tell a two billion-year old story of the earth's history. Finally, there is the role that humans have played in the story for thousands of years. Those who have called the Canyon home – the Hualapai, Havasupai, Southern Paiutes, and the Navajo Indians – left behind plenty of cultural relics that we enjoyed on our hike, such as the mysterious split-twig figurines and fascinating petroglyphs carved into the rocks. There were many times during my hike when I was so overcome by the immensity, history and beauty of Grand Canyon, I cried. (Grand Canyon information supplemented by Wikipedia)

Grand Canyon has two rims. The North Rim and the South Rim are just ten miles apart as the crow flies and 215 miles apart by road. The South Rim, which is open all year, has an average elevation of 7,000 feet. The North Rim, open from mid-May to mid-October (snow closes it in the winter) has an average elevation of 8,000 feet. There is a small window of opportunity each year to complete a Rim-to-Rim hike. (Wikipedia)

Rim-to-Rim-to-Rim hikers (South Rim to North Rim and back to South) are granted the ultimate experience: well-constructed trails, maximum views and unsurpassed geology lessons. I was an R-to-R-to-R hiker and was cautioned early in my planning that I had a two-month-long window to complete my hike – too early and I might be battling waist-deep snow; too late and I would have to contend with the Canyon's infamous heat. I decided on the last week in November, which turned out to be the first week in December because of difficulties "Roughin' It" had of obtaining a camping permit in November. It was even colder than I expected it to be because of storm conditions that moved into the Canyon that week; we encountered snow, high winds and low temperatures.

We used the South Kaibab Trail at the South Rim to descend to the bottom of the Canyon on the first day, and then the North Kaibab Trail to ascend to the North Rim and back to the bottom. On the last day, we used the Bright Angel Trail to return to the South Rim.

Phantom Ranch at the bottom of the Canyon is reachable only by foot, mule or raft (several companies provide helicopter tours). I learned that if one would like to stay at the lodge and enjoy a $44 steak dinner, he/she should make reservations a year in advance. Since we were "roughin' it," we didn't avail ourselves of these material luxuries. However, what we were given – and accepted–was the luxury of seeing both the North and the South Rims at the same time from the bottom of the Canyon. There are few experiences more spectacular than that!

"Roughin' It" emphasized the importance of being physically and mentally fit for the Rim-to-Rim-to-Rim hike. The elevation change of more than 5,000 feet to the bottom, combined with the weight of a 38-pound backpack, can do serious damage to one's feet and knees. Then there's the 5,000 foot hike out of the Canyon which occurs at the end of the hike when hikers are mentally and physically drained...... the last quarter mile to the top was extremely painful for me.

Not only the Company but people who had completed the hike warned us not to have high expectations which could break us down mentally. Ninety- nine percent of the people who have backpacked Grand Canyon said that the hike turned out to be harder than they thought it would be, and those who rated themselves an 8 out of 10 on the "Roughin' It Fitness Scale" finished their hike rating themselves a 3!

This is the Fitness Rating Scale provided by "Roughin' It:"

1) Couch potato
2) Golfer who rides a cart
3) Mall walker
4) Golfer who walks and carries clubs
5) Gym member (3-4 days a week)
6) Serious gym member (5 plus days a week)
7) 8), 9), and 10) marathon runners with at least one marathon per week (10)

Those who rated themselves a 5 or a 6 on the scale were assured that they would be able to do the hike with the right preparation and training. I trained hard and prepared extensively – did everything "Roughin' It" told me to do – and rated myself a 6. I barely made it to the top on the last day.

I think the most important piece of advice I was given was to not sacrifice the views, sights, and sounds of the moment for anticipation of the ending. At the same time, I was told to keep in mind that the goal was to finish – actually, there was no option other than to finish.

Grand Canyon is sacred to many people so rules have been established for hikers that are always enforced. Most of the rules exist for the preservation of the environment. The ones that directly applied to us are the following:

- All trash must be carried out. "If you pack it in, pack it out." It's the No Trace Principle.

We used compost outhouses when available (had to pack out the toilet paper), and when outhouses were not an option, we had to make sure that we deposited our waste at least 200 feet from water, camp and trail. We stored our food and trash in aluminum containers and hung our backpacks in trees so rodents and other animals couldn't chew through.

- Wood or charcoal fires of any type are prohibited as are fossil fuel backpack stoves. Our guide used a little sterno backpack stove to cook all of our one-course meals. Unfortunately, that little stove couldn't provide the heat I needed so badly during the long nights of shivering.

- Use of biodegradable or any other type of soap in creeks within 100 feet of any water source is prohibitive. We washed ourselves and our dishes at faucets that were at least 200 feet away from streams and used very small amounts of biodegradable soap.

- Removing from its natural state any rocks or archaeological resources is prohibitive. We examined but didn't touch cultural relics and left rocks, plants and other natural objects as we found them. An exception was a few little stones for my granddaughter which the park service gave me permission to remove from the Canyon. (Information on rules from "Roughin' It" literature.)

We were cautioned to remember that uphill hikers have the right of way, and downhill hikers have to yield to them – and to the mules. We tried not to talk loudly as we hiked, knowing that natural quiet is a treasure in Grand Canyon. Actually, we had no trouble refraining from energy-sapping conversation and obeying the 8 p.m. to 6 a.m. quiet period at our campsites.

"Roughin' It" stressed the importance of eating carbohydrates and drinking plenty of fluids at least one full day before the hike. I consumed a healthy portion of delicious pasta prepared by my daughter-in-law the night before I departed for Grand Canyon. I became almost obsessed with my food-water intake on the hike, having been warned repeatedly that either water intoxication (too much water and too little food, creating an electrolyte imbalance) or dehydration can be debilitating. I made myself eat a small amount of mostly salty foods and drink water about every half hour, regardless of my level of thirst and hunger.

While "Roughin' It" supplied us with everything we needed for the hike, each of us was responsible for carrying and taking care of the following:

- Tent. Mine was a one-person tent that was too small for any kind of movement and came with a zipper that had a tendency to stick. The tent was inadequate for the extremely cold, wet weather we unexpectedly encountered.

- Mat. I had to unpack, inflate, deflate and pack my mat inside my tent – not an easy task, given the tight quarters and the intense cold which prevented my fingers from working well.

- Sleeping bag. This I also had to set up inside the tent, a task even more difficult than the mat. It was a small bag and I felt like an encapsulated mummy with absolutely no room to maneuver once I wiggled myself inside. Manufactured to endure 15 degree temperatures, it didn't keep me from freezing every night, probably because of the wild wind chill.

- Head lamp and crampons. These items were necessary for hiking in the dark and snow and I wore them, but not with confidence. I found the head lamp especially to be intimidating and didn't trust it to keep me on the trail.

- Meal tin. We ate all of our meals in a compact tin, consisting of a plate, bowl, cup and utensils. After each meal, we washed these in cold water, sometimes without soap. There were a couple of times that I didn't wash them at all because my hands were too cold to subject them to freezing water.

I remember reading in the "Roughin' It" literature that we would have to swallow our pride in terms of our appearance on the hike – that we would be sore, sweaty and dirty but so would everyone else. "You can do anything you set your mind to as long as you keep it real." I still laugh about this because my appearance was the least of my worries on the hike. Yes, I would have liked to look better than I did for photographs that were later seen by the rest of my world, but at the time I didn't care about how I looked, only about how I would make it back to the top of the South Rim.

While I was hiking, I experienced a few nervous moments when the narrow trail forced me to walk too close to the edge. I thought about how easy it would be for me to lose my balance or my footing and plunge over into the abyss. I experienced real fear when we encountered a part of the North Kaibab Trail that had eroded, leaving us a tiny ledge that we could use for crossing. The National Park Service had strung a rope alongside the canyon wall that we held on to while side stepping across. I was scared to death the first time we had to cross that section when we were going up to the North Rim. The crossing going down was less frightening because I had already proven I could do it.

When I asked our guide about fatalities in the Grand Canyon, he characteristically acknowledged them but downplayed their significance, other than to comment that "accidents do happen." It was only when I bought a book at the South Rim bookstore at the end of the hike that I realized my guide's comment was a little too cavalier. The title was a dead giveaway: *Over the Edge: Death in Grand Canyon*, published in 2001 by Ghiglieri and Myers. The book chronicles a comprehensive history of fatal events in Grand Canyon. While reading it, I kept thinking that I was glad I found the book after my hike, not before.

Ghiglieri and Myers document four kinds of deaths in Grand Canyon: falls from the rim; lethal events within the Canyon; suicides; and murders. There have been 55 accidental lethal rim falls from 1925-2012. A fall from either rim mostly occurred when people failed to pay attention to warning signs or did not use common sense; these falls almost always equaled death. People who had no sense of danger- or just wanted to show off–posed for the ultimate picture on the very edge, leaned over to get a better look, or nonchalantly strolled along narrow, rocky paths at the rim as if they were in a shopping mall. In one fatality, for example, a father wanted to impress his daughter by playing hide and seek on the rim. At one point, he pretended to fall to scare his daughter and then really did fall 400 feet to his death. When he didn't emerge from the bushes, his daughter ran to her mother who notified the National Park Service. The rangers found his mangled body, hidden in a crevasse, after several days of searching.

Most of the lethal events within the Canyon from 1880 – 2012 have been environmental deaths (93) caused by cardiac arrest, heatstroke, hypothermia, and dehydration. The majority of these deaths occurred with backpackers who were either hiking without a guide or were hiking with a guide who exercised poor judgment. In 2009 alone, a record ten hikers died due to arrogance, poor judgment, and reckless behavior. Everyone who is planning to hike Grand Canyon would be sadly remiss if he/she didn't make it a point to become thoroughly informed about the real dangers the canyon wilderness poses and always will pose.

There have also been 45-50 accidental falls within the Canyon during this period. Ghiglieri and Myers point out that accidental falls by hikers within the Canyon bear almost no resemblance in their conditions and victims to the falls of tourists from the rim, probably because hiking into the canyon, and then getting back alive to tell about it, demands a high level of skill. Hikers who died from a fall while hiking the Canyon are those who either didn't possess the required level of skill in the first place or made bad decisions that resulted in their death.

Stories abound about the gigantic risk taken by people who attempt a rim- to-river hike down the South Kaibab Trail and back up on the Bright Angel Trail in one day. This warning is particularly – but not exclusively –important for older people who can die of cardiac arrest combined with dehydration. An NPS ranger found a message on a Blackberry from a young hiker who had attempted a one day rim-to-rim hike and gotten lost on a lesser known trail. He was dying from dehydration (heatstroke) and wrote: "I feel like going into the wild is a calling all feel, some answer, and some die for."

Warnings also are widely distributed and communicated about the danger of hiking in Grand Canyon during months of excessive heat. A 68-year-old woman (my age!) hiked nine hours from the South Rim to the Colorado River (with plans to dine at Phantom Ranch) and then continued on against the advice of trail experts. Temperatures in the Canyon exceeded 100 degrees and she had drunk less than two quarts of water. She collapsed near the Kaibab Suspension Tunnel (a mile from Phantom Ranch) of heat stroke and died with a core temperature of 104 degrees.

People also die from hypothermia hiking the South Rim to the North Rim, most of the time in the months of January and February. Because of the unusually cold weather during our hike the first week of December, I was convinced that hypothermia would be my death sentence. Every morning, after a night of shivering, our guide conducted the "finger test" for hypothermia and assured me that I would live to see the day.

About 80 suicidal deaths below Grand Canyon rims have been recorded from 1914-2013. According to Ghiglieri and Myers, what makes suicide in Grand Canyon an important issue is its uniqueness of offering a "spectacular, sure-fire (almost), easy and even a 'Heaven-sent' opportunity to end it all." This opinion seems to be supported by the three independent copycat suicides in 1993, the year of the movie "Thelma and Louise." Since it became possible for vehicles to have access to the rims, eight cars have driven off them.

The actual number of people who commit suicide in Grand Canyon is fewer than one would expect. Five times more people than those who committed suicide were those who were killed accidentally, due to air crashes in and around the Canyon (65 fatal crashes of various aircraft). With both kinds of fatal events, the NPS rangers and the Coconino County SAR have to recover bodies or body parts and, in doing so, expose themselves to highly significant danger. However, while accidents are unpreventable, suicides can be prevented, and the National Park Service encourages people who are contemplating suicide to not come to Grand Canyon. "If you are contemplating suicide, please do not come to Grand Canyon, thus risking the lives of rescue personnel and sabotaging the well-being of others......call 911. The old aphorism that suicide is a permanent solution to a temporary problem is usually true. Changing one's mind in midair rarely works out."

The last category of deaths in the Grand Canyon is murder which almost never happens. Considering that more than half a million people have run the Colorado River in Grand Canyon, and over a million more people have hiked or camped within it, the very low number of 25-30 known murders within Grand Canyon, or on its rims, is impressive. According to Ghiglieri and Myers, the first murder took place in the 1800s when the husband of a Navajo refugee family killed an outlaw who was caught in the act of butchering the horse that the husband's pregnant wife had just been riding. The last documented murder took place in 2001 when a 30-year-old woman was found stabbed to death under her bed. The motive or reason for her murder has never been determined.

Probably the most infamous Grand Canyon murderer was Robert Spangler. In 1978, he murdered his wife and two teenage children so that he would be free to marry his new love who hiked the Canyon with him. The marriage ended in divorce. When Spangler's third marriage went sour, he pushed his wife off a 140-foot drop while hiking in Grand Canyon. He detailed all four murders to investigators before he died of brain cancer in prison in 2001.

Our guide was calmly competent and thoroughly knowledgeable about the history of Grand Canyon and the potential dangers of hiking within its walls. He advised, but didn't coddle (an action that I appreciated, given my age!). Having been a wilderness guide for 20 years, he had a great number of stories to tell about people who under his care had experienced various degrees of distress. He shared a few, and I think the stories he shared were carefully chosen so as not to instill fear in us. After reading *Over the Edge,* I was grateful for his restraint.

Depending upon the set of statistics being examined, there have been 685- 706 accidental and non-accidental deaths within Grand Canyon from 1860- 2012. But there has been a shift in what kills people. In the last decade, most of the deaths were of people who died from environmental problems, mostly succumbing to heat, and there are more people dying from falls within the Canyon as opposed to falls from the rims. There are more suicide jumps from the rim and more drownings from boaters on the Colorado River.

I wonder why people do dangerous things, especially when they are aware of the potential for something to go very wrong. When I asked this question of a friend who climbs mountains, he said, "It gives my life meaning." Another friend told me that he takes risks with his motorcycle for the rush and, to some extent, for bragging rights. For me – if I were in the habit of doing dangerous things–I think the answer would lie somewhere in the realm of needing to prove something.

The Six-Day Hike

December 1, 2013. The day had come! My son drove me to the Holiday Inn in Phoenix where I was supposed to be picked up by my Grand Canyon guide at 4:30 a.m. I had slept only two hours and was feeling nervous about the consequences of so little sleep, given the physical task that lay ahead. When Jared failed to show up, I became increasingly nervous and talked myself into believing that I had the wrong meeting place or the wrong time. I kept thinking of reasons why a 67-year-old woman shouldn't be doing a Rim- to-Rim-to-Rim hike in Grand Canyon.

Jared finally arrived at 5:10, and we left the Holiday Inn to pick up the other hikers at their hotels. Initially, our group consisted of Jared, two guys from Mississippi and me. At the last minute, however, a young couple from Singapore joined us, so now we were six.

We drove in the dark to Flagstaff where we stopped at a backdoor café for the best coffee I have ever tasted. Jared and the others bought breakfast, while I ate the delicious breakfast burritos my daughter-in-law had made me. My companions kept eyeing my burritos so I offered to share one of them.

I had an ulterior motive for my generosity, thinking that in sharing I could endear me to them so they would want to offer assistance on the trail should I need it. Based on the introductions and table conversation, I knew that I was the oldest among us by far………given that fact, it didn't require much imagination to think I might need some help on the trail!

Because of our late start, we didn't get to the South Kaibab Trailhead until 11:00. After packing and weighing our packs (mine weighed 38 pounds), we finally hit the trail at 11:30. My nervousness returned. I knew we had to descend 4,800 feet and 7.4 miles to get to our destination at the bottom of the Canyon, hopefully before dark. Given an average hiking time of six hours, beating the darkness was unlikely.

I had trained for almost a year and now my Grand Canyon experience had become a reality. All of my hard work was about to pay off. The hours I had spent at the gym, working with heavy weights to strengthen my body and running on the treadmill to improve cardiovascular fitness; trudging around my neighborhood breaking in my boots and carrying a backpack filled with 30 pounds of flour; searching for hills and inclines to give me a feeling for what it would be like to ascend and descend…….. I was prepared and ready to go.

When I took my first steps down the trail, I couldn't dissolve the lump in my throat. I don't know which emotion was stronger, my excitement or my amazement – 67 years old and I'm hiking down the South Kaibab Trail to reach the bottom of Grand Canyon and the Colorado River!

South Kaibab is a thru trail taking hikers from the South Rim to the bottom of the Canyon and then continuing north on the North Kaibab Trail, ending at the North Rim. The trail is on an exposed ridgeline, so we were surrounded by breathtaking, wide open views which made us very much aware of the vastness of the Canyon as we descended. We followed the top of the ridgeline and felt the Canyon warming up fast until we were at the total mercy of the sun. There was little shade and no water available at any point along the trail. My need for warmth at the rim was quickly replaced by the shedding of layers in order to be comfortable lower down.

The size of everything and the space of it all was staggering. We carefully descended the tight switchbacks of the Chimney, and then the trail opened up to afford a view of "Ooh Aah Point" – appropriately named because of the overwhelmingly spectacular panoramic views. The trail continued to follow the top of the ridgeline until it led into the Devil's Staircase, also appropriately named because the plunging switchbacks were steep and treacherous.

We made it to Skeleton Point, and I think it was there that we rested at a popular mule train stop. The mules had delivered supplies to Phantom Lodge and were now on their way back to the South Rim. (Mules are indispensable to the Grand Canyon, both for carrying tourists and transporting supplies.

Everything needed at Phantom Lodge, including the beef for the popular $44 steak dinner, is carried there by mule. The trash is carried out the same way.)

After our brief water and rest stop, we hit the trail again. Suddenly (or so it seemed), the trail blasted out of limestone cliffs, exposing us to Nature in her abundantly colorful best. All around, there were juniper growing out of the rocks, wildflowers, and different colored layers of sandstone and limestone.

Beautiful light patterns in the Canyon walls shown between dark clouds and sunshine. I wanted to clap my hands and shout for joy, but that kind of enthusiastic response could have sent me over the edge. I had to concentrate hard on stepping just right on the three-foot wide timbers that were laid across the trail to accommodate the mules and prevent erosion.

My knees had started to feel sore, but they were still working. It was when the trail started descending rapidly and we had to manage another series of steep switchbacks that my legs were really feeling the pain. I kept reciting a mantra that I had learned: keep my knees bent and step through my heels. I think that the trekking poles, which I had no trouble using, saved me because they redistributed some weight from my legs and onto my upper body. I also decided to do something about my backpack which kept shifting and needed constant adjustment……I had to push it back in place, making walking difficult. I asked Jared to look at it, and he fixed the straps so my pack stayed in place. I thought it was strange that he hadn't thought to check my pack before leaving the rim, knowing that I was inexperienced in backpacking.

Jared cheerfully announced that we were on the final descent to the bottom of the Canyon. The Colorado River swirled below me and, even though I was more than 1000 feet above it, I could hear the roar of the rapids. It was getting dark and I was tired, but my spirits were buoyed by the knowledge that the end was near.

We reached the River Trail intersection at 6.4 miles in the dark. I put on my headlamp and instantly felt insecure in my ability to use it. I was sure that it would fail me and I would fall or go off the trail. A few more switchbacks and we entered the 50-foot long tunnel that empties out onto the black suspension bridge (Black Bridge) which hovers above the Colorado River. When Jared informed us that it was still a half a mile to the Bright Angel Campground, I had to will my tired body to continue and constantly reassure myself that the terror I felt about my headlamp was misplaced.

We arrived at the Bright Angel Campground on the Colorado River at 6:00 and had to set up our tents and sleeping bags in the dark, since no wood or charcoal fires are allowed in the Canyon. Jared cooked our dinner in a little pot on his camp stove, and we ate in the dark. No one felt much like talking because we were all hungry, cold, and exhausted. After washing our tin plates and cups in icy water, we stored our food in ammunition containers on the table to keep the critters out and hung our backpacks on a tree to discourage those that decided to visit us in the night.

I crawled into my tent and the nightmare began. By the time I got my pajamas on, I was freezing but believed that I would warm up as soon as I crawled into my sleeping bag. Within minutes, my socks went back on, then my shirt, followed by my hiking pants. When I had donned every piece of clothing I owned – over my pajamas – and still felt cold, I knew I was in trouble. Sleeping has never been my forte, and now I was at the complete mercy of an unfriendly environment. I shivered uncontrollably all night and didn't get any real sleep. I realized that, while I was prepared for the physical aspect of the trip to be harder than I expected, I hadn't planned on the bone- chilling cold.

My sleeping bag, which was supposed to be good to 15 degrees, failed to protect me from the freezing cold and I laid awake, shivering and obsessing about my inability to hike tomorrow with no sleep. I willed myself to stop shivering; I prayed that I would stop shivering; and when neither will nor prayer worked, I became scared. I fixated on a tingling sensation that I was sure I felt and panicked because this false sensation of feeling warm is what severely hypothermic people experience just before they lose consciousness (I had read that). The last time I picked up my flashlight to look at my watch, it was 4:15. I must have slept then for a couple of hours before I heard voices outside my tent telling me it was 6:30 and time to hit the trail. I had made it

through the night! What is it that someone said……
the best work is a slog, then it's done and you say, "I
did it! It was terrifying, but I made it!" That's the way
I felt.

Sunrise on the canyon walls is other – worldly.
The first rays strike the majestic canyon walls and
make their way down until they flood the valley
floor, allowing a view of even more of the canyon's
splendor. It was one of those million dollar mornings
and, despite a lack of sleep, I felt good, inside and
out. Jared said that today would be "a walk in the
park" to prepare us for the grueling hike to the top
of the North Rim tomorrow. He turned out to be
right. We spent an hour at Phantom Lodge where I
wrote out some postcards that mules were supposed
to carry to the rim. We also filled up our bladders
with the last potable water on the north side of the
river; everything after that would have to be filtered
from Bright Angel Creek which runs along the North
Kaibab Trail. My last view before leaving Bright
Angel Campground was of several mule deer grazing
near the camp, and I took that as a good sign.

Our destination today was Cottonwood
Campground, the halfway point on the North Kaibab
Trail. The North Kaibab Trail is 14 miles long with
an elevation gain of 5800 feet and passes over Bright
Angel Creek several times on little bridges. The seven
miles between Phantom Ranch and Cottonwood

Campground are at a relatively low elevation. We ascended gradually up the Inner Gorge, through "The Box," a narrow canyon within the Canyon, where the trail is boxed in on either side by massive cliffs of red wall which have sent huge blocks of stone down to line the trail. Jared explained that we were hiking in a 1.7 billion- year-old Vishnu Schist where over one billion years of geology are missing. I saw a lot of evidence of the ancient civilizations that once called Grand Canyon their home…….. could feel the weathered soul of the Canyon in my increasingly tired bones.

As I worked my way up Bright Angel Canyon along the swiftly flowing creek, I realized, to my relief, that my body didn't seem to mind the lack of sleep, and I was able to enjoy the 1600- foot ascent and the diverse ecosystems around me. The box canyon passed quickly as I sauntered along, immersing myself in the day that was unfolding before me. I even led the group for most of the four hours it took us to arrive at our next campground!

We arrived at Cottonwood Campground around 4:00 and actually had time to set up and eat before it got dark. There wasn't much at Cottonwood – just tap water, the campground, a ranger station that wasn't manned, and a compost toilet a short walk from the campgrounds. The sunset was magnificent – an orange glow surrounded the canyon and our campsite. I felt euphoric. But that feeling was short-lived: Jared announced that snow was in the forecast and temperatures would drop to 20 degrees with an unusually high wind. I hadn't fully processed that piece of bad news when two backpackers descending from the North Rim reported tough going. Despite my nervousness, I tried to stay positive as I prepared for the night.

Once again, I found myself spending a long night shivering, even though I was wearing every piece of clothing I owned, plus a wool scarf that Jared had given me. My mind fixated on the belief that I was slowly succumbing to a hypothermic death in a tent pitched deep in Grand Canyon with a sleeping bag designed to withstand temperatures no colder than fifteen degrees (with no wind chill factor!). I had read about hypothermia as part of my training for this hike, so I knew that it is an unpredictable, gradual and insidious death. I began to shiver uncontrollably. At one point, my muscles were shaking so hard I was sure that the noise could be heard outside my tent. I prayed that the shaking would stop, and then I prayed that it wouldn't because it was my body's method of buying time in the hope that the temperature would rise, or enough heat would be generated in my shivering to slow the drop in temperature. I knew that shivering is the first of several progressive stages of hypothermia, followed by weariness, heavy movement, a distorted sense of time and distance, and confusion. In the end, the victim is thoroughly disorientated and prone to hallucinations. I knew that if I were, indeed, hypothermic, my situation would get worse, and eventually my body's reserves of fuel would run out and the shivering would stop, thereby increasing the rate at which I would freeze. I would slip into a coma and my heart would cease to beat. I would mercifully sleep. I prayed frequently and fervently that my shivering wouldn't stop.

In my most lucid moments, I realized that I was not going to die. But I couldn't shake the scenario, and I even left my tent to take a walk in the cold night, hoping to deflect dying thoughts. I looked for the toilet which was farther away from our campground than I had thought, so I squatted along the path. When I returned to my tent, I couldn't get in because the zipper was stuck and I didn't dare pull too hard, in the event that I would rip it and have to survive with an open flap. By the time I got it open, I was so cold that I didn't climb into my sleeping bag at first. I remember thinking that it would be easier for me to pack up in the morning if I didn't have to extract myself from such tight quarters. Eventually, I got in…….. and laid there, alone with my shivering thoughts, prayers, and worries about the next day. I think it would have helped if I had been able to take along the book I had packed, but Jared insisted that I leave it behind in the car because of the added weight. Reading by flashlight would have provided some comfort and made the time go faster. I tried writing in my journal but my gloved hands were too cold and bulky to form letters.

I made it through a second night.

Note: Even though my companions admitted to being cold at night, they slept in double tents and were able to derive body heat from each other. I was the only one with a single tent. Jared slept on the ground in a sleeping bag that was designed for freezing temperatures.

On Monday we were standing at the top of the South Rim; yesterday we were at the bottom of the Canyon; and tonight we found ourselves at the top of the North Rim! We hiked seven miles in seven hours and ascended 4,200 feet on the North Kaibab Trail. I started off well but became increasingly tired during the last hour. The only thing that kept me going was the promise of sleeping in a yurt that night. And we did………but more of that later.

From Cottonwood Campground it is 6.8 miles uphill to the North Kaibab trailhead and an additional 0.2 miles further to the yurt. Our first destination after leaving Cottonwood was the Pumphouse Residence, only 1.5 relatively easy, stunningly beautiful, miles up the trail. The Pumphouse Residence is both a pumping relay station and a watering hole. It serves the trans-canyon pipeline which is buried beneath the North Kaibab Trail. (We saw it as it stretched across the Colorado River, under the Bright Angel Trail's Silver Bridge.) The pipeline provides water throughout the Canyon, including the South Rim.

A Grand Canyon employee named Bruce Aiken lived here for decades, taking care of the pipes and pumps. In addition to his role as caretaker, Aiken was also a painter who used his spare time to capture the grandeur of the ever-changing Canyon. I was told that hikers coming down from the North Rim years ago could look forward to quenching their thirst with a cup of ice cold lemonade sitting in the shade of an old Cottonwood next to the caretaker's garden. (I wouldn't have minded a glass of lemonade, just thinking about the hardest part of the day's journey ahead of us.)

Upon leaving the Pumphouse Residence, the trail narrowly skirted red rock cliffs and climbed precipitously. However, we were rewarded for our hard work with some of the most spectacular views in the Canyon. Jared kept cautioning us not to think about this part of the trail as being the most difficult, since the hardest was yet to come.

Our next landmark was Roaring Springs, a thundering wall of water which shoots straight out of solid rock on the opposite side of Roaring Springs Canyon. We were at an elevation of about 5,000 feet which meant that we still had over 3,000 feet to go. I couldn't help but notice that the North Rim still towered overhead and wondered if we could possibly make it to the top before dark. My legs and lungs were in pretty good shape as we passed the last bridge crossing Roaring Springs Canyon, but I was tired.

Just before we reached the Supai Tunnel, Jared suggested a rest stop on a huge rock in a shallow cave looking out over the Canyon and a couple miles of the trail we had covered. It was a beautiful spot to rest and gain some respite from the blazing sun......

and to prepare for the steep ascent to the Supai Tunnel, which marked the end of the massive cliffs of Redwall, the deep layer of red limestone that we had been grinding upward forever, it seemed.

It was a steady battle, but when we emerged from this small, man-made tunnel cut through the rocks, we were treated to an imposing view of the cliffs and switchbacks that we had conquered below us. We were on the final stretchonly 1.7 miles to the North Kaibab trailhead.

I soon discovered that Grand Canyon had saved the best (worst) for last. We were almost at the North Rim as evidenced by the ponderosa pines, snow banks at the side of the trail and high winds. But I thought we'd never arrive. I was almost at the point of exhaustion. If it hadn't been for my hiking poles, which took some of the stress off my legs and allowed me to use the upper body strength I had built up in training, I think I would have succumbed to the temptation to lie down on the trail and let the elements have their way with me. It was getting dark so we donned our headlamps and strapped on crampons to manage the ice and snow on the narrow trail. I still didn't trust my headlamp to distinguish the trail from the edge, but the crampons seemed to improve my grip on the ice and snow….. I guess success with one out of two pieces of equipment managed to make me feel a little more secure about conquering the steep, never-ending switchbacks and gradually making progress to the rim. I kept thinking that it can't be that much farther now.

When I took the last few steps to the North Rim and arrived at the sign for the North Kaibab Trailhead, I felt an overwhelming sense of accomplishment. I was standing on the North Rim of Grand Canyon at 8,241 feet and feeling on top of the world!

The North Rim yurt was a ten- minute walk on level snow-covered ground from the North Kaibab Trailhead. In Grand Canyon, the yurt can be reserved during the winter months when the North Rim is only accessible by hiking across the Canyon. The octagonal structure accommodates six people and is outfitted with a table, chairs and a wood-burning stove.

I loved our miniature house immediately! Everyone scrambled to make a fire in the little wood stove and claimed spaces around it. We wound our headlamps around our water bottles to make a satisfying glow in the hut, which was so small our sleeping bags touched as we laid them out. A trip to the portable toilet revealed a spectacular sky, studded with stars so large I endured my aching body and the freezing cold just to watch them for a while. The heat inside the yurt was delicious, and I could hardly wait to lie down and sleep. I fell asleep instantly but was jarred awake a couple of hours later with a familiar body reaction: intense shivering. The guy next to me was also shivering, so I knew it wasn't just my problem this time. We had let the fire in our little stove go out, and it took a long time to gather enough wood to build another one. We did get the fire going, but by then I was wide awake, and sleep eluded me until morning's light. I was disappointed that I couldn't sleep several hours but feeling warm was enough of a good thing. While still dark, we packed up, turned on our headlamps and strapped on the crampons, feeling not so eager to step into the morning cold. Before we left, the ranger (only person up there besides us) knocked on the door to find out if we were all right. He told us that it was 15 degrees below zero.

We left the yurt in pre-dawn darkness, wearing headlamps and all of the warm clothes we possessed. It was brutally cold..... my fingers froze almost immediately. But the quiet beauty of the canyon was compensation for my physical discomfort. The hike down from the North Rim began as an evergreen forest that reminded me of Northern Minnesota. Before sunup we had descended to the Cococino Overlook where we were treated to a wonderful showcase of Cococino sandstone overlooking the red rocks of the Supai formation. Light gradually filled the sky around 7:30 a.m. The dawn, fresh snow and Redwall offered an amazingly beautiful sight which couldn't be captured by pictures or even held by memories. But I'll always be able to recall how incredibly blessed I felt at that moment to be a part of such unbelievable beauty.

We continued in the Ponderosa pine forest, descending through varying ecosystems as the elevation changed the landscape around us, until we reached the Supai Tunnel about two miles into the hike. We passed through the tunnel and emerged into a desert environment. The descent was very steep (dropped about a mile over the course of a five-mile hike). Even though going down the North Kaibab Trail wasn't easy, it wasn't as hard as going up so I was able to enjoy the ecosystems this time.

Because of the cold and the hiking difficulty, it took me about an hour on the trail for my body parts to work together again. When we were safely past the worst of the snow at Supai Tunnel, my legs started working pretty well, and I was able to pick up my pace so I didn't lag behind the others. I felt good about that because for most of the ascent yesterday, I was fifth in line, with only Jared behind me. It was hard to ignore the negative effects of the age difference between me and my companions, and I was forced to admit that sometimes age does matter when it comes to physical demands of the body. However, I was very pleased with how well my legs, arms, and lungs were serving me overall……. and I felt extremely grateful.

A hiker I had met at Phantom Lodge suggested that there was something defeating about return trips. He said that once you make it to the top, you just want to get back to the starting point. Now that I had been to the top and was making my way down again, I strongly disagreed with his point. The familiarity I gained about the trail while ascending allowed me to enjoy the spectacular views now on my descent because I wasn't so distracted by the physical exertion of the ascent.

We made the 4,100 foot, seven-mile descent on the North Kaibab Trail to Cottonwood Campground in five hours. After enjoying moderate temperatures on our descent in the Canyon, we were cold again and shivered through dinner and camp set-up. Jared felt sorry for us (even though he also was cold), so he made us tea and hot potato soup as soon as we arrived. I can't tell you how delicious the packaged soup was! Then he announced that we were going to have a Thanksgiving dinner which, of course, caused images of turkey, mashed potatoes, stuffing and cranberries to dance in our heads. We wondered how he was going to pull that off, though, since all of our dinners had been "one pot" conglomerations. Well, we did dine on all of the traditional Thanksgiving foods…….. combined in our pot. It tasted good, and I wanted more but there was none. It seemed as if there was never enough food to fill me up. I think the others felt that way also. We wanted seconds but having them would have resulted in a lot less food for Jared. (I think the reason we seemed never to have enough food is because two people joined at the last minute and "Roughin' It" didn't have the time to adjust quantities.)

Thirty to forty mile an hour winds, combined with snow and temperatures of 15 degrees yielded another sleepless night. Almost 12 hours shivering again in a cold sleeping bag with no one to talk to except God….

By the way, when the going got really tough during the day, I repeated my favorite mantra: "This is my job today. I can either do it well or I can mess it up." It helped move me forward.

The hike from Cottonwood Campground to Bright Angel Campground was relatively flat, but it had its challenges, including the length (7.2 miles). We passed through "The Box" again, and this time the immensity and beauty of the vast labyrinth of canyons was so overwhelming I could hardly breathe. I thoroughly enjoyed my walk through the geologic past. After the Box, which is the narrowest part of the lower canyon, we emerged into a series of relatively open terrains, with occasional ups and downs and stunning unobstructed views.

We hiked along Bright Angel Creek all the way to the campground, with a stop at Ribbon Falls, which is located near the bottom of the canyon and a little ways off the North Kaibab Trail. Instead of following the well-travelled trail to the falls, we crossed the creek and found our own way. It was a short cut which required us to jump on rocks in the rushing creek to avoid getting our boots wet. That was the intent, but I slipped and fell into the water twice; the second time water filled my boots so that I squished when I walked. I could hear the clear sound of the falls as we crossed the creek and followed a faint rocky path with small elevation……then it was another five-minute walk to Ribbon Falls.

We gazed up at a jet of water spouting out of the high canyon wall and spilling down a brilliantly green 50-foot rock face. I was transfixed by the narrow ribbon of water dancing from side to side across the moss-covered dome of Ribbon Falls....... it was magnificent!

We had ridgeline hiking, with unobstructed stunning views, most of the way down to Bright Angel Campground. Because of the relatively easy terrain and elevation, walking required little concentration so I lost myself in the Canyon, overcome by its immensity and beauty. I was struck by my good fortune: How is it that I am so blessed as to have this opportunity to walk through the most spectacular geologic past in the world?

We arrived at Phantom Lodge in a little over four hours and had fun sharing conversation and comparing notes with other hikers. It was hard for me to completely relax because I couldn't shake the nervousness I felt about having to climb out of the Canyon back to the South Rim the next day. Jared mentioned that everything we've done up to now has prepared us for the rigors of the last day. I kept thinking that my lack of sleep has to eventually produce some deleterious effects and tomorrow would be the day of consequences. Remarkably, I've felt no ill effects of four sleepless nights....... very grateful. My legs and feet have served me so well that I haven't had to use any of the products I meticulously packed before I left: Moleskin, toe covers, Advil....... I haven't even opened the packages. I thank the good Lord for my strong body and for the opportunity to rigorously train for eight months. I'm also thankful to the guy who persuaded me to buy expensive hiking boots instead of the cheaper pair I had picked out….. this was one time when I'm convinced that high quality was worth the high price!

While talking to the owner of the Cantina, we found out that the dormitory had a few empty spots, a discovery that put all of us in the uncomfortable position of weighing the importance of a good night's sleep against staying true to our roughing it status. Four of us opted for the dormitory rooms, ultimately not caring if the luxury of sleeping indoor qualified as cheating. It seemed as if everyone had some level of anxiety about the next day; my level was probably the highest.

As it turned out, I was warm and comfortable (no shivering) but sleep didn't come easily. It eluded me most of the night, I suppose because of worry and the comings and goings of people who were turning on lights at all hours.

There was a knock on the door at 4:30, signaling that it was time to go. I didn't want to wake the other occupants, so I tiptoed around in the dark, retrieving my things and filling my water bladder. I thought the four of us were going to walk to the trailhead together, but the others had already gone by the time I was ready. The darkness was unnerving, especially since I was unsure of the direction I needed to take to get to our meeting place, which was some distance away from the dormitories. I passed by campsites I didn't recognize from the night before; in fact, nothing was familiar, and my nervousness increased with every step and night sound. Just when I was convinced that I was going the wrong way, I heard Jared's voice and saw the outline of his body, motioning me to proceed.

It was 5:00 when we assembled at our campsite for breakfast and departure. There was no enthusiasm and minimal conversation. We packed our backpacks in the darkness of the Canyon. I'm pretty sure that all of us were thinking the same thing: Today is the ultimate test. Am I up to it?

The morning didn't begin well. I couldn't find my mess kit so I had to eat cold cereal without milk; my headlamp needed new batteries, which were hard to find; I realized I had forgotten to take my blood pressure medication; and I felt jumpy. When Jared asked if I was all right, I felt like crying (so didn't want that to happen) but nodded instead. He assured me that I would make it to the top….. and we left.

I hit the moonlit trail with heavy feet, sucking in the cold air and very much aware of the babbling brook and the whistling wind. The darkness unsettled me and, even with the new batteries, I was convinced that my headlamp would fail and I would topple over the edge!

The route back to the South Rim along the Bright Angel Trail starts out across the Colorado River on the Silver Bridge, and then follows a sandy path alongside the river on a fairly easy up-and-down slope for more than a mile before turning and heading up the rim. This is where the River Trail ends and the Bright Angel Trail actually starts. It moves away from the river on a mild grade and crosses the creek several times. I tried to turn off my headlamp a few times in the early morning hours to see if I could get along without it, but I didn't trust my footing in the loose, thick gravel. I was so happy when the trail lit up in the orange light of the rising sun. It was promising and beautiful!

Despite my inauspicious beginning, I felt surprisingly good and eager for the final climb. I had read that, while the route down from the South Rim on the South Kaibab Trail follows a ridge line and is all about big views, the route up on the Bright Angel Trail follows the head of a side canyon, framing the views with massive cliffs and giving the trail a sense of intimacy. I was already feeling that intimacy………

Note: According to the National Park Service, the Bright Angel Trail is very much like the route used for millennia by the many Native American groups that have called Grand Canyon home. Originally an Indian trail used by the Havasupai Indians to commute between the rim and Indian Garden, the trail was improved by prospectors in the late 1800s and extended to the river. It became a one dollar toll road before the National Park Service assumed ownership in 1928 and provided tourists with free access to the river.

A couple of miles after we turned on to the Bright Angel Trail, we hit the Devil's Corkscrew, a set of serious switchbacks that climb up the side of the Canyon. Along with the steepness, I had trouble maneuvering the steps built to accommodate the mules. While I welcomed the logs on the way down the South Kaibab Trail (I stepped on each log to give my feet a little bit of an uphill sensation), I now hated them on the way up because climbing across them interfered with steady walking and sometimes it seemed like just too much effort. The poles helped, but the mules grind the gravel to sand which makes the poles harder to use. We encountered a mule train with tourists going down to Phantom Lodge and two empty mules heading down the river for emergency evacuations of river rafters. There were massive amounts of green mule dung on parts of the trail, but I didn't mind that since I had to watch my footing anyway. Mule trains are a constant fixture on the Bright Angel Trail and they always have the right a way, so we had to stay on the inside of the trail until they passed. At one point during the passing, the mules appeared not to like me and engaged in a behavior that I found to be nerve-wracking: stomping nervously, swaying their heads, and sprinting wildly past, as I tried not to get trampled. Jared told me not to take their behavior personally!

The Devil's Corkscrew was a killer, and I was happy to hear the news that we were moving into the Indian Garden area with a gentler grade because my legs were begging for some relief.

After several creek crossings and about three miles of hard hiking, we arrived at Indian Gardens. It was truly the oasis everyone said it was….. giant cottonwood trees, cool shade, fresh spring water, pit toilets, and more squirrels than I could count, running all over and pausing in front of us in anticipation of a few crumbs. I consumed a huge chunk of summer sausage on a dry bagel and refilled my water bladder. While sitting on the bench, I noticed a wooden bulletin board explaining how horrible our death would be from any number of causes: dehydration, exhaustion, sunstroke………all of this illustrated by the drawing of a man lying prostrate from his hike down the canyon. I couldn't help but think that this sign should have been posted at the trailhead!

I could see the full profile of the South Rim from Indian Garden. Knowing that the big climb was ahead of us – 3,000 feet, over 4.5 miles – I wanted to stay at this oasis and just gaze at our destination. I entertained thoughts of not really being able to get up there.

After Indian Garden, the Canyon walls and the grade got steeper as I climbed higher. The switchbacks at Jacob's Ladder seemed to go on forever……unrelenting. My pace slowed down and I concentrated on every little detail of the trail, choosing the best place for every single step. The only comfort I derived was looking back to see the trail snake back and forth below me. It was a reminder of how far I had come. I found myself looking back often, and the view became an antidote to defeat.

The distant vistas and wide horizons propelled me forward.

I slogged on, stopping often to soak in the serenity of the Canyon—the changing colors and the sound of the ravens I found to be intoxicating. My mindset wavered at times as I became increasingly fatigued, but I never strayed from my goal: There was only one way to get to the top and I had to do it. Energy came and went in waves; sometimes I had to stop and look around because I couldn't will my body to continue. I just wanted to rest.

We finally arrived at the mile-and-a-half rest house……1200 feet below the rim at an elevation of 5,700 feet. I needed a toilet break badly and was horrified to discover that the pit toilets were a couple of hundred feet from the trail! Someone surely had a warped sense of humor. Jared reminded us that we had only a mile and a half and 1100 vertical feet to go. The bad news was that this final section of the trail was steep, by virtue of the topography of the Canyon, and was notorious for defeating climbers with its unrelenting steps that keep going up. Called "Heartbreak Hill," the name accurately describes the task that lay ahead. After hiking eight miles already, I knew that I would have to summon all of the strength I had left in order to get to the rim. If that wasn't enough to dampen our spirits, Jared said that the weather would not be good………a storm was moving in with snow and cold temperatures.

My legs finally rebelled. They turned rubbery and then started cramping. I had to stop at every switchback to give them a 20-second rest. With less than a mile to go, I began to doubt that I might make it all the way up to the top. I believed that I was close to finishing, but when I rounded a corner, I saw more switchbacks and no end to the trail. The light was fading quickly in the side canyon, and I couldn't feel my knees. Then it started blowing snow, and I had to put on my crampons because I couldn't see the ice underneath. My companions forged ahead of me, wanting to get to the top before the blizzard. Jared stayed with me, encouraging me at every switchback: three fourths mile to the lower tunnel; a quarter of a mile later, the upper tunnel. Above me loomed the rim. For a split second, I thought about my Everest challenge so many years ago and prayed that the ending would be different this time.

We were a half a mile from the top when Jared announced his decision to go ahead to prepare for the trip home in blizzard conditions. He reminded me to stop and look at the petroglyphs carved into the rock above us and then assured me that I would make it. I wanted to ask him not to leave me but I nodded my head and said, "Okay" instead. Before he left, though, he did something wonderful. He took my hand and said, "Judy, your sons should be very proud of you." That's all. Then he left. I think it was at that point that I sat down on a rock to watch the canyon fill up with snow. It was a magical sight, and I thought about just lying down and going to sleep.

When I finally reached the top of Bright Angel Trail in a blinding snowstorm, I couldn't find the lodge and there was no one around to tell me how to get there. I yelled for help (only once because I immediately felt embarrassed) and stumbled around until I could see it in the distance. I tried to compose myself and wipe some of the snow off me before I opened the door, but a woman saw me from inside and rushed over to guide me to the restroom. I barely held it together until I was alone and then the tears erupted. The emotions I had packed deep within myself for the sake of survival knotted up in a lump and rose to the back of my throat. I indulged in a ten- minute cathartic cry and then went to the gift shop to buy a Rim-to-Rim-to- Rim t-shirt, only to be told that there weren't any because "no one does that hike." I wanted to slap the salesperson but, instead, bought a Rim-to-Rim shirt with the idea that I would add another "Rim" myself.

I found my group seated at a corner table in the café, already eating bison burgers with all the trimmings. I ordered the same thing. We ate in silence……for a while all that was heard was the sound of eating. Everyone, including myself, seemed to be lost in thought or too tired to talk. I wanted to ask why no one was concerned when it took me so long to find the lodge – why no one came out to look for me in the snowstorm – but knowing the answer to my question didn't seem worth the effort it would take to ask. My burger was unbelievably delicious.

Just as we were leaving, one of the guys in my group told me that there actually were some Rim-to-Rim-to-Rim t-shirts hidden in a corner of the shop, collecting dust. I went back to the shop and found one……bought it even though it was ugly and worn looking.

I climbed 9.5 miles, almost 5,000 feet today! It took me a little over eight hours to accomplish that. I wish that I had had someone to share my exhilaration when I reached the top, but it was okay. Only the blizzard heard me yell, "I did it!" When I stood at the South Rim, though, as tired and cold as I was, I saw the world differently. I remember thinking that anything that might seem impossible in my life from this point on, I just may be able to do. I heard someone say that adventure is defined as when you are doing it, you pray to God to get you out alive, and when it is over, you ask Him to let you do it again. I want to hike Grand Canyon again.

So that's my story. I walked 45 miles and ascended and descended a total of 23,000 feet. I endured brutally cold temperatures, sleeplessness, and hard work for six days, and my body rebelled only at the very end. I witnessed a kaleidoscope of colors in the magnificent formations of one of the world's wonders. I felt God's greatness in the vastness of Grand Canyon. I have been richly blessed.

Note: I learned in a conversation with personnel from the National Park Service that Grand Canyon experienced an unusual weather phenomenon the week of my hike. A weather inversion trapped fluffy, white clouds below the rim, allowing visitors to the South Rim to be above the clouds and view amazing red rock formations through the clouds. For hikers, however, this was not a good thing. The warmer air masses from above trapped colder air masses in the canyon, causing penetrating cold that made hikers freeze. The early blizzard was a surprise to everyone. I've always thought that I expect a lot of my body and it had always delivered. Grand Canyon was no exception. However, subjecting it to the brutal cold of Grand Canyon without enough protection may have been asking too much. Every night I created a mummy bag in my tent and slept with every piece of clothing I had brought with me and still couldn't stop the shivering. I guess my heart simply failed to keep all of me warm.

Resting on the South Kaibab Trail

Phantom Ranch

Sunrise in the Canyon

Freezing at Cottonwood Camp (not my tent)

The yurt

Mule sign at the North Rim

The magnificent colors
of Grand Canyon

Ribbon Falls

Last day on the Bright
Angel Trail

Snow storm close
to the South Rim

Back to Phoenix and Home

After inhaling our bison burgers, Jared urged us to hurry so that we could start for Phoenix as soon as possible because he was worried about the blizzard that was showing no signs of abating. He had already re-packed the bag I had brought with me to the trailhead with personal items from my backpack – everything that didn't belong to "Roughin' It Adventure Company." The others had packed their bags while waiting for me to finish the climb. Without telling me anything about the location of the van in the parking lot, Jared and the rest of my group left the restaurant while I went to the restroom. I felt stupid – and embarrassed–walking blindly around the parking lot, looking for the van. I realized that Jared's actions were motivated–and probably justified – by his concern for getting us safely back to Phoenix in blizzard conditions. He was in a hurry and most likely just forgot to tell me where the van was parked. Nevertheless, I felt a sense of abandonment for the second time, and the whole scene was disconcerting.

Our four-hour ride back to Phoenix was characterized by little conversation and no camaraderie. While I didn't mind the silence – I was used to it by then–it occurred to me that my experience shouldn't end like this. Shouldn't we have felt some kind of bond that would make us want to celebrate? Where was the "We did it!" excitement? Why weren't we congratulating each other? Shouldn't we be feeling elated at having completed an adventure of a lifetime? Maybe we were all too tired, or maybe we just didn't feel any group cohesiveness. We talked about wanting to establish future communication, and even passed a sheet of paper around to share email addresses, but the attempt was feeble, as were the goodbyes when each of us left the van.

I called my son when we were a couple of hours from Phoenix (we had left the storm soon after Flagstaff), and he was at the hotel to meet us when we arrived. I had never been happier to see him! I thanked Jared for a fantastic experience and tipped him an amount of money that was suggested by the company. He told me I had done well and to keep in touch. That was my final goodbye to Grand Canyon.

I don't remember what I said on the ride to his house, but my son told me later that I was cold, hungry, and relieved to have made it back, so I must have said those things. When we arrived, I know that my little granddaughter and my daughter-in-law were happy to see me. I also know that I luxuriated in their ultimate shower for a long time and ate bowl after bowl of the best chili in the world! Instead of going to bed right away, which I was expected to do, I stayed up until we all went to bed.

The next morning, I ate another bowl of chili and spent time with my granddaughter, admiring the Christmas tree and playing "Pesky Pirates." I gave her the few lovely stones I had received permission to remove from Grand Canyon. I remember thinking that the scene was normal in a surreal way.

My husband was at the Detroit airport to meet me and, instead of immediately going home, we stopped at our favorite gathering place where I devoured a whole pizza. For the next several days, I couldn't seem to get enough to eat, but I didn't sleep any more than usual. Bill said that he was proud of me.

If I had known what would be involved in hiking Grand Canyon, would I have done it? When asked why he wanted to climb Mount Everest, George Mallory famously answered, "Because it's there." That quote has become, some 90 years later, a popular answer to the provocative question asked of anyone attempting extraordinary things. So why did I do it? I can think of several lofty answers to that question: It was a way of seeing how far I could take myself at the age of 67; it simplified my life for a short time; and I experienced personal growth in that week. I suppose my answer to the "why" question contains a bit of truth from all of the above. Or maybe I hiked Grand Canyon because it's there.

It was the ultimate challenge. I had to constantly push myself – there were times when I had to put everything I possessed into the task of making one step upward or downward. But hiking Grand Canyon was a glorious and life- changing experience, and there was no better feeling than coming home after having done it. And Grand Canyon more than delivered. It has left me deeply enriched by its immensity and sheer beauty. I will always remember – and carry with me forever – its magnificence.

Reflection
(December 6, 2014: one year after Grand Canyon)

Nostalgia grabs hold of me these days – not so much for my Himalayan experience which I'll never be able to recapture because of my age, but for my Grand Canyon experience which I would like to replicate and feel that I may be able to do so, in some fashion. I seem to crave adventure and physical challenge as much now, at 68, as I did when I was young….. maybe more. I want to start training for something again – what, I'm not sure, but I'm going to train anyway. I was happy when I was training for Grand Canyon and felt lost when it was over. I liked the purposefulness of training, the routine, the singular goal, and the opportunity to push my body as far as it would go. I liked being forced to train so that on days when I didn't feel like going to the gym, I went anyway because I knew that my planned adventure depended upon a strong body.

At the same time, I know that I'll have to slow down someday and acknowledge the wear and tear on my body which makes risk-taking more difficult – but not impossible! I want to embrace adventure as late into life as my body will allow. I really want to be an intensely active older woman, absolutely determined to enjoy life for everything it has to give – always thinking possibilities instead of limitations; always a little hungry to get off the beaten path.

I can't remember a time when travel hasn't been important in my life. Except for the fact that I can't travel the same way now that I'm old(er), nothing much has changed. I remember fondly the travel days of my youth when I'd decide on a destination and then look for creative (and inexpensive) ways to get there. Once there, I'd settle in a youth hostel and then walk around, looking for cheap places to eat and talking to anyone who was interested in listening to me. When I felt that I had exhausted the possibilities in a particular place, I'd hop on a train, not really caring where it was going. In Europe one year, I used a Eurail Pass to sleep on the train and then get off at one of its morning stops, not caring where it was. It was a wonderful time in my life, a time that I could have because I was young, with no responsibilities other than keeping myself alive and well.

Well, I can't travel that way anymore……… haven't been able to do so since I began a career and became a mother. And then we have the old age thing. There's something about old age that invites a desire to settle for a time, long enough to get to know a place and the people. I'm thinking that I'd like to spend some time on the West Bank in Paris and write a novel at Select, the café where Hemingway wrote "The Sun Also Rises." I'd like to go there every day at the same time so the owner will bring me my cafe crème without having to ask for it. It doesn't have to be Paris; it could be Ireland or Norway, New York or Alaska– places I'd love to get to know better. But Paris seems to be a logical choice for becoming a regular in a café.

On a recent trip to Norway to visit relatives, I realized something about myself that may be relevant to aging: my reticence to try new things, in this case, speak Norwegian. When I was in Norway at 18, and again in my 50s, I was eager to use what little Norwegian I knew, and felt a sense of pride at trying to communicate with my relatives in their native language. This time, however, I spoke all English and was even willing to watch my older relatives struggle to communicate or not communicate at all. I was angry at myself and fearful that this one instance of reticence would permeate other aspects of my life. Was I losing my nerve to try difficult things? My guess is that I was unwilling to take the risk of sounding ridiculous instead of focusing on the fact that my relatives would have appreciated any attempt to speak Norwegian on my part. The sad fact of the matter is that there really wasn't any risk.......

Unfortunately, I'm starting to realize that the greatest effect of time and aging is memory. It's increasingly happening in my life where I remember events by their context and not by the details. It distresses me to realize, for example, that I can remember my granddaughter singing "Let it Go" while we were in Phoenix and can place her doing this on the front patio at her house. What I can't retrieve from my stubborn (fading) memory are her facial expressions and expansive gestures, details that made the event so precious. Photos help, of course, but they don't capture everything. I just have to keep grabbing moments and challenging my memory to be definitive with regard to those moments.

It may be that I'll keep reinventing myself as I pass through the years. I know what I've been able to do in my 60s – what my 70s, 80s and beyond will bring, I don't know. I'm already mulling over possibilities for my next adventure. Maybe I'll try white water rafting, helicopter skiing, or a different backpacking experience. Perhaps I'll pursue further exploration of Grand Canyon, hiking lesser-known trails and more remote parts. Maybe I'll hike the Superior Trail or return to the idea of hiking parts of the Appalachian Trail, or even find a way to thru-hike the 2100 plus miles. Maybe I'll travel to an exotic and remote wilderness destination. I might even overcome my nervousness about the ocean depths and take scuba diving lessons. Whatever action I decide to take in the next few years will involve commitment and mental and physical preparation, so I'll keep training. I will also be praying that I can find meaning and joy in life at any age. What I will try not to do is see myself as forever young, in the literal sense, even as I stop pretending that I'm okay with the aging gracefully philosophy. I will most likely "rage at the dying of the light" for the rest of my life.

Postscript

Since completing this manuscript and preparing it for publication, I have marked the entrance into my 70th year by completing another adventure and falling in love again with mountain hiking. Three friends and I embarked on a self-guided, three-day, inn-to-inn hike in Rocky Mountain National Park. The experience consisted of spectacular hiking during the day and sleeping in comfortable lodges at nights. No freezing nights locked in a small tent set up on hard ground for me this time!

We enjoyed a splendid first day of hiking from Aspen Glen to East Portal, a total of seven miles with an easy 1500 foot elevation gain. The trail crossed three beautiful meadows and afforded us spectacular views of the Rocky Mountains. I hadn't been able to train as much as I wanted to for this trip and felt a little nervous about my body's ability to climb the rocky grades, but it didn't take long to establish a hiking rhythm which worked well, even on the steep parts. While taking us to the trail entrance, Phebe (company owner) taught us the "rest step," a technique which prevents a hiker from feeling exhausted too quickly by focusing on the foot he's not stepping down with, so it's a step-down-pause motion. It worked for me.

We arrived at our B&B in the afternoon and had a delightful time exploring the Western ambience of Eagle Cliff House. Unfortunately, there was one unwelcomed reminder of my Grand Canyon experience: a sleepless night despite the warmth and comfort of an inviting bed. I experienced more than a little *déjà vu* in the concern I felt for my second day of hiking which, according to reports, would be more difficult than my first.

And it was. As a matter of fact, the second day was as tough as any day of my Grand Canyon hike, except for the last day when I had to climb 5,000 feet to the South Rim. We left Estes Valley on a trail that climbed steadily to Storm Pass. It took us over ten hours to hike nine miles and ascend 2700 feet to 10,300 feet at the top of the pass. Three of those hours we traversed the side of the mountain on snowshoes, and another two hours we ski poled because the snow was so deep. Since we were the first group to hike across Storm Pass, and virgin snow still covered the relatively new trail, Phebe decided to go with us. She knew the way and kept us moving at a slow even pace. I didn't think that I would have a lot of trouble snowshoeing, having done it before, but I was so wrong. The technique we had to use for staying on the side of the mountain was different from the technique I was used to for level terrain: Mountain snowshoeing required us to plant the steel claws at the top of the snowshoe in the snow and concentrate on each step. I broke concentration at least twice to reap the consequence of falling and sliding down the mountain. One of my falls was convincing enough to make me think I wasn't going to be able to get back on the trail. The other hikers fell also, but my fall topped everyone else's......twisted legs and buried snowshoes! Phebe kept reminding us to look back at the views from where we came, and I was somewhat comforted both by the beauty and the feeling of accomplishment. After a while, I felt secure enough with snowshoeing to practice the rest step technique without miss-stepping too much.

We made it past Storm Pass, and I thought the three-mile trail down to Lily Lake where we would be staying for the night would be relatively easy. The trail did wind its way down to Lily Lake, but there was still quite a bit of snow in areas that impeded our progress, mostly because it was even more difficult to use snowshoes in the descent than it was in the ascent. Eventually the snow left us and we were treated to an interesting change in landscape. I kept thinking that the plentiful supply of moose droppings on the trail (those little brown footballs) surely meant that we would have the pleasure of an encounter with that majestic animal, but it never happened.

We were two hours late in arriving at our destination for the night, and the person who had been assigned to meet us at the end of the trail confessed that she was a little worried. We piled in the van and made it to our wonderful 1917 Victorian lodge called The Baldpate Inn just in time to meet the dinner deadline. We devoured our soup and salad quickly so that we would not miss out on the much-anticipated pie that was touted to be the best in Rocky Mountain National Park. We were not disappointed!

Despite ideal sleeping conditions and a body that was beyond exhausted, I didn't sleep much again………worrisome because I thought my Grand Canyon ordeal was the result of freezing every night and, without that component, sleep wouldn't have been a problem. Now, I realized that my sleeping problem is more complex. I spent the nighttime hours reading and writing in the comfortable lobby.

I finally went to sleep for a couple of hours and woke up at 6:30, feeling tired and creaky. We had been told that the best had been saved for the final day of our hike. Since nothing could be more challenging and interesting than yesterday, I imagined that the "best" had to refer to scenery and possibly easy enough hiking so that we could fully enjoy our surroundings. I was right. After eating a hearty cowboy breakfast and blow- drying my soaking wet boots, I was raring to go.

It was the loveliest of days. Since the hiking was considerably easier than the day before, we were able to savor the deep lush forest, the rushing streams, and mountain views on the trail up to Calypso Cascade. After that, we split up so that I hiked with Phebe across a beautiful meadow to Allenspark where we met the others who had taken an alternative route. We hiked a total of seven miles with an elevation gain of 1800 feet.

We stayed the night at a classic 1930s log lodge. The proprietors of Allenspark Lodge, Juanita and Bill Martin, were lovely hosts who did everything they could to make us feel welcome, including making sure that coffee, hot chocolate, water and high altitude tea were available at all times. They also provided an early (4:30!) morning alarm clock: two roosters, Al and Bert, who crowed magnificently. We were the only diners (first of the season) at the Fawn Brook Inn, a lovely restaurant with a European ambience, a five-star chef, and a young waiter who aimed to please. The owners, a Swiss/German couple in their 80s, want to sell the restaurant so they can retire, and our waiter wants to buy it but is having a hard time coming up with the money. I wished him well.

Gazing at our destination

"Just follow Phebe"

The mighty fall

Made it to Storm Pass

The Baldpate Inn

With this postscript, I end my book. As the old hymn says, "I know not what the future holds but I know who holds the future." I really do hope that God grants me many more years of good health and strong legs, because I have several adventures I'd like to pursue. I'm pretty sure they will all involve hiking, either mountain or long-distance or a combination of the two. I'm thinking about the Superior Hiking Trail or the Katy Trail in South Dakota………and, perhaps one of these days, I'll do the Irish or English coast to coast trails. The possibilities are endless.

As for this being a book about aging………well, the reader can decide for himself (if the question is at all interesting), but I've come to the conclusion that it isn't. While my views on aging are quite obvious (I think), there isn't enough of a focus on the topic to qualify as the theme for my book. What I set out to do was describe two extreme adventures that I've had in my life, one when I was young and the other when I was older, with the idea that anyone reading this book would discover that there was a great deal of similarity between the two adventures in terms of what my mind and body were able to do, despite the 41-year age difference. Since my mind and body were able to endure difficult challenges at both ages......... doesn't that discovery reflect a message about aging?

The author and her granddaughter
in Phoenix after Grand Canyon.

www.ingramcontent.com/pod-product-compliance
Ingram Content Group UK Ltd.
Pitfield, Milton Keynes, MK11 3LW, UK
UKHW022210230426
12048UKWH00016BA/756